British
Columbiana

British Columbiana

A Millennial in a
Gold Rush Town

Josie Teed

DUNDURN
PRESS

The names of some individuals in this work have been changed to respect their privacy.

Publisher: Kwame Scott Fraser | Acquiring editor: Julie Mannell
Cover designer: Laura Boyle
Cover image: woman by istock.com/Master1305; mountains by oksmith

Library and Archives Canada Cataloguing in Publication

Title: British Columbiana : a millenial in a gold rush town / Josie Teed.
Names: Teed, Josie, author.
Identifiers: Canadiana (print) 20220431299 | Canadiana (ebook) 20220431329 | ISBN 9781459750210 (softcover) | ISBN 9781459750227 (PDF) | ISBN 9781459750234 (EPUB)
Subjects: LCSH: Teed, Josie. | LCSH: Wells (B.C.)—Social life and customs—21st century. | LCSH: Wells (B.C.)—History. | LCSH: Tour guides (Persons)—British Columbia—Barkerville Historic Town—Biography. | LCSH: Self-actualization (Psychology) | LCGFT: Autobiographies.
Classification: LCC FC3849.W43 Z49 2023 | DDC 971.1/75—dc23

We acknowledge the support of the Canada Council for the Arts and the Ontario Arts Council for our publishing program. We also acknowledge the financial support of the Government of Ontario, through the Ontario Book Publishing Tax Credit and Ontario Creates, and the Government of Canada.

Care has been taken to trace the ownership of copyright material used in this book. The author and the publisher welcome any information enabling them to rectify any references or credits in subsequent editions.

The publisher is not responsible for websites or their content unless they are owned by the publisher.

Printed and bound in Canada.

Dundurn Press
1382 Queen Street East
Toronto, Ontario, Canada M4L 1C9
dundurn.com, @dundurnpress 𝕏 f ⓘ

For Darien and Deb

Chapter 1

DAD INSISTED ON TRAVELLING WITH ME WHEN I GOT THE job. I was to be the curatorial intern at Barkerville Historic Town & Park for six months from October 2018 until March 2019. The head curator emailed me to tell me that the person they offered the job to first had turned it down, and so it was mine if I wanted it.

It was both hurtful and exhilarating to be someone's second choice for the role, and to be told this by the person who made the decision. This was the type of mean information adults shared with each other all the time. For instance, I knew that many Oscar winners had been the second choice for their winning roles. Even Julie Andrews had been passed over for *My Fair Lady* after originating the role of Eliza Doolittle on Broadway, only to win for *Mary Poppins* the same year. I told myself I could be like that.

Barkerville Historic Town & Park, a preserved gold rush town, is located in the Cariboo region of British Columbia on the western end of the Rocky Mountains, halfway between Washington State and the Yukon.

I had never heard of Barkerville before and I only conceptually understood that it was very far away. It took an entire day to drive from Vancouver. I couldn't imagine anyone I knew going there, and it was difficult for me to picture a car leaving a city and travelling into interior British Columbia. What could that possibly look like? How could a city fall away to mountains and thousands of acres of wilderness?

However, I wanted to work in museums, my "chosen field" following my master's, and I hadn't received any other job offers. It paid $22.50 an hour, almost eight dollars above minimum wage, because the position was so remote. It had to be partially subsidized by the government because nobody wanted to live there. I had little idea of what a good salary was, but this seemed too promising an offer to refuse.

I was offered the position two weeks before I flew home to Ontario. I was completing my master's degree in medieval archaeology in York, a small city in the United Kingdom. I was to go home to Fenwick, Ontario, which was twenty-five minutes from Niagara Falls and two hours from Toronto. People often asked me if I saw the falls all the time and if they were beautiful. I always replied yes because it made people smile, and when I said no it made them frown. I was going to spend a few days in Fenwick with my family, and then fly to British Columbia. My accommodation would be in Wells, a town ten minutes outside Barkerville, in the "staff house" that a few employees could rent for $500 a month if they didn't have their own place to stay.

From my laptop in my already packed up apartment, I googled "Wells, B.C." and opened the Wikipedia page.

In 1942, it had a greater population than Quesnel or Prince George. The closures of the gold and other mineral mines in 1967 took their toll on the town and most of the population moved away. Today it has a listed population of just 250 which doubles during the summer months.

I read on. "Wells has a subarctic climate." "July daily mean: 12.3 degrees Celsius." The prospect of living somewhere that had a population of only 250 people, and that was so cold, concerned me. Perhaps these conditions would teach me something about human nature and the essence of life itself that my peers did not know, and I could, for once, carry on confidently assured that I held a great secret about living well. I was also sure that spending a year in England and then six months in rural British Columbia would signal to everyone — my parents, whose approval I desperately sought, and my classmates at McGill, many of whom had already landed in miraculous careers as if by magic — that I actually had a lot going on, had found my way to that narrow road toward success, and was definitely an interesting person worthy of their respect and admiration.

I learned that Wells hosted an annual art and music festival in the summer called "ArtsWells" that attracted a hundred thousand people. I learned that the arts organization, Barkerville, the adjacent Bowron Lake Provincial Park, and the existing mines employed almost everyone in Wells. I followed another link to a Facebook group called "Wells, B.C. ~ an artistic community."

"The community of Wells, B.C., is looking for creative individuals to move to our community." The cover photo was a white woman with a pixie cut in a carnivalesque outfit standing on the shoulders of a man dressed like a court jester. They piggybacked in front of a parade of smiling faces marching down the streets of Wells.

My whole life people had been telling me I was creative, but this photo seemed diametrically opposed to who I was. Would I be surrounded by these people in costumes at some point if I moved to Wells? Was this inevitable? How would I feel then: happy, like the woman, or pained by embarrassment, like I currently was looking at her photo? Was that woman even happy? I closed my laptop.

My last few days in England were all the same. I would wake up, pick up three pre-packaged white-bread sandwiches from the Sainsbury's on the corner of my street, and journey through a field of cows to campus to work on my thesis. After eight hours or so, when I couldn't write anymore, I'd make my way home again and watch five hours of *Love Island* until I fell asleep.

I was supposed to be writing my thesis on medieval archaeology, but I'd struggled for a long time to think of anything to say. I'd been starting to suspect that I wasn't all that interested in medieval archaeology, but that could not possibly be true because I had sunk myself into incomprehensible debt to study it.

All my classmates found old doorknobs and soup ladles fascinating and revealing about the social, political, and economic conditions of both the past and the future, and even after a year I did not. They used exciting, charged language to describe buttons found in trash deposits from 950 CE, which never would have occurred to me to use. As much as I wanted to be like this myself, it all bored me, the dendrochronology, the peat bogs that I read about but never got to see, and the promise of Norse shield-maidens who never materialized in the evidence.

Exhausted by my choice, I'd told my supervisor that I really just liked movies.

"Why don't you write about medieval buildings — on film!" she had said.

"What do you mean?"

"You could study the relationship between depictions of medieval buildings and the reality."

"I don't understand how that could be considered important."

"Oh, it would certainly be important." She waved her hands vaguely from behind her desk as she said this but didn't elaborate further.

My supervisor was the foremost scholar of medieval guildhalls in England, and so I regarded her as a trustworthy authority on what was important and unimportant in medieval archaeology, but also in life.

While I was working on my thesis in those last few days, I caught the worst cold I'd ever had. My throat and nose were so plugged with phlegm that I vomited in the middle of the night. And yet something about the idea of pushing my body and mind as far as they could go before crashing was pleasing to me. When I spoke with people on the phone, I said that writing my thesis was taking its toll on me. It was invigorating to say that and actually mean it. I timed my cold medicine so I didn't overdose. In the U.K. it came in a liquid form called Lemsip, which tasted like hot Kool-Aid.

I submitted my thesis at 9:00 p.m. on the last possible day. It was the middle of September and my flight to Toronto was at 7:00 a.m. the next day. I slept for three hours, and then took a cab to the train station and rode to Manchester. On the plane, my ears plugged up immediately with congestion and never unplugged, even when we touched down in Toronto.

Delirious from travel and medication, I cried on the car ride home and told Dad he needed to take me to the hospital because my ears were damaged. Dad just smiled at me, unsure how to respond. We went home and my ears were clear when I woke up in the morning. With my faculties newly restored, and finding myself back in my childhood home, smelling cat dander on my childhood pillow and coffee from the kitchen, my time overseas began to feel like a strange dream.

The next week, Dad and I took two flights to get to Wells: one five-hour flight from Toronto to Vancouver, and another to Prince George, which was just over an hour. The second plane was small and reminded me of Howard Hughes. We had to board the plane directly from the tarmac, like fighter pilots going to battle. There were twenty seats. In front of me were two young Indigenous men. Both of them were very tall, and they were speaking to some elderly people across the narrow aisle. From their conversation I learned they were rappers and travelled to different reserves and towns to perform and to talk to children.

Dad listened to the men, too, and he turned to me and raised his eyebrows quizzically. The look on his face said that he was thinking something but didn't know if I'd be receptive to it. Because I was tired and irritable, I said, "What?"

"Nothing," Dad replied, shaking his head, still smiling. He is a champion of unnecessary poker faces.

The plane took off differently from other planes I'd been on. It shook like it would crumble against any wind and turbulence, as if a successful flight would require the calmest of conditions.

Dad, a frequent flyer, wasn't concerned. He fell asleep almost instantly, his head cocked back and his mouth open as if waiting for the dentist.

I gazed out the window. We were flying over enormous mountains. I had never seen mountains like that before — they didn't exist in Ontario or England or Quebec or anywhere else I had travelled. Clouds shaded the peaks, and I was overcome by the distinct feeling of being underwater, as if beyond the ring of white puffs was where some truer plane existed, an unknown world that was larger, more magical, and closer to God than anywhere else.

As time passed, I wondered if I had misunderstood the geography of British Columbia somehow, if the entire province was a singular mountainous mass. Eventually things changed. The mountains became greener, and soon everything was covered in forest, then field, then forest again. Some areas resembled desert. We never got very high in the little plane, so I could make out pastures full of cows, tractors, specks of people, and pickup trucks.

Things nearer to Prince George were browner. There were ugly buildings lurking in the shadows of Mother Nature, dry ground and razed forests.

"Those right there are paper mills, Josie," Dad said, pointing to one of the brown buildings. "Paper is a big industry in northern B.C." Dad loved to research the places he was going, and I was sure that, like me, he had read through the Wikipedia page for every stop on our trip.

"Wow," I said, although I had already guessed as much.

• • •

We landed at the tiny airport in Prince George.

Outside, it smelled like burning garbage. I waved my hand in front of my nose and made a face at Dad.

"Ahhh, that'll be the paper," said Dad. "Stinky, right?"

We drove into the city in a rental car, and the smell continued, at times intensifying and then dulling inside my nostrils, coming back stronger each time.

Before we left home, Dad had found a car for me to buy in Prince George. We arrived after 5:00 p.m., so we had to stay the night in a hotel and pick up the car in the morning. Jet lagged, we fell asleep in our respective beds on either side of the hotel room early.

At 3:00 a.m., I woke up. Looking over, I saw that Dad was also awake. We made eye contact. I closed my eyes, and when I opened them again it was morning.

7

We picked up my car at a used car lot. It was a shiny red Chevy Cruze from 2011. Inside the dealer building, I scanned a roster of licence plates, eventually choosing "CPP AB1." *See pee pee abeeone,* I thought.

Dad had the crazy idea that I would drive alone to Wells, and he would drive in a rented car in front of me. I knew this was gratuitous and unnecessary and I could just go on my own and leave him here to wait for his flight, but I was actually terrified of arriving in Wells alone, so I went along with his plan. We left Prince George, Dad driving slowly in front of me.

In my car for the first time, I put on a premade playlist called "40s Country," which I'd listened to almost every day while writing my thesis. I liked it because it was refreshing, and consistent, and I felt like I was learning something about the past by listening to those old, long-dead voices, who couldn't know that they sounded nothing like voices do today.

Many of the songs featured a woman singing backup in a hilarious, high-pitched tone, like Mickey Mouse. I almost suspected it was the same woman in every song, but that couldn't possibly have been the case.

The music exactly suited the landscape and vice versa. We were, after all, in "The West," and all of the album covers that flashed on my iPhone screen showed white men in cowboy hats.

Since accepting the job, I had been considering the notion of "The West" very carefully. I thought that, although it was a common genre of film, no one really paid much attention to the fact that the west was not some big homogenous thing. Some Westerns were set in Oregon, and some in Texas, and some Alberta, and some Washington state, or Nevada.

I suppose the stories were all the same: a representation of the idea of manifest destiny, and later in post-Westerns, subversions of it. Is that the only thing these places had in common? That, and cowboy boots and mud and cows and horses and some misguided notion that they deserved to survive out there because they were stronger than other people?

It occurred to me that I was driving directly into one of those iterations of manifest destiny. Would I be disgusted? Or would I be enchanted and fall under its spell like all of those Italian filmmakers?

In high school, I watched a lot of Westerns, whichever ones I could get my hands on. I had never seen the 1957 *3:10 to Yuma*, but I had seen the remake with Russell Crowe and Christian Bale. My favourite was *The Assassination of Jesse James by the Coward Robert Ford*. It was so slow and well-shot, and there were many close-ups of men's faces revealing anguish and humiliation and other secret, masculine emotions.

To get to Wells, we had to drive south out of Prince George to Quesnel, an hour and a half away on the big highway. This was easy enough, as we only had to go straight, although the logging trucks were incredibly aggressive, and more than once I was sure I would be driven off a cliff or into a muddy ditch.

We stopped for groceries in Quesnel. I couldn't think of anything to buy, and I picked out five cans of soup, orange juice, pasta, a carton of eggs, and some cans of tomatoes. As I browsed, I felt a growing, unexpected panic. I became painfully aware of being between situations. It was mortifying: Dad knew me, and would see me transplanted into an entirely new place, where no one knew me. He would almost certainly see me meet other people. In fact, when I thought about it, he wouldn't leave until I had met another person. This idea was overwhelming. I didn't think I could successfully bridge my old self, the one that Dad knew, with the self I wanted to present to other people I didn't yet know, and with whatever vague dream I had of who I could become in the future. I thought I would faint, like a traumatized woman in a Victorian novel, knocking boxes of cereal and ketchup bottles onto the floor.

Being back in the car was a relief, but it was short-lived. We turned onto a small road with a steep incline. Our route was winding, and I was terrified. The car seemed to be gliding, and I thought at any moment the steering wheel would take on a life of its own, driving me off the steep cliffs that gradually revealed themselves to me as we journeyed inland.

In Wells the air did not smell like paper mills anymore, but like trees. We were greeted in our cars by an enormous and friendly looking welcome sign in yellow with red trim. The town was surrounded by softly curving mountains on three sides, which were green, not grey, covered in pine trees punctuated by bursts of deciduous orange. On the third side was a marsh, which gave way to more hills and mountains. As we entered the town proper, the first thing I noticed was the Jack O' Clubs General Store, which was also a gas station and a restaurant and bar. It was imposing, and sported a big black club painted on its front face.

Dad pulled over to the side of the road, and I followed. We got out and surveyed the area together. The air was cold and clean in my lungs, like breathing a glass of water. There was a harshly evident quietness, but I wondered if that was true, or if I was just trying to meet my own expectations.

Before going to the staff house, Dad and I drove a loop around the town in our respective cars. I'd searched Wells on Google Maps before arriving. There were two sides of town, one on each side of the highway: the charming side where the Sunset Theatre, the Wells Hotel, the local school, and the fire department were located. And the other side, where the staff house was, and which contained fewer homes and more mining buildings. I had worried that this could somehow affect my social life and that the "charming side" people might exclude me from social events.

Dad and I stopped at the Wells Hotel because he was very taken with photos he had seen, and he had learned through research that there was a quaint bar inside. He couldn't stay the night but wanted to go look. I wondered if he was sad to have booked a flight for the same evening, but I was too shy to ask him about it.

The Wells Hotel was a large yellow stucco building, with a brown roof and big yellow arches leading to the reception. An old man loitered outside, smoking a cigarette. I locked my car, and when he heard the beep he smiled like he was an actor in a perform-ance: he moved his cigarette hand meaningfully and said, "You'll be offending people if you're going to be locking your car. I think you'll find we do things a bit differently here." He raised his eyebrows expectantly and nodded at me.

To deny him the pleasure of a reaction, I attempted a neutral smile that was really just a stretching of my mouth to the sides of my face. Dad and I peeked inside the bar together, feeling sheepish. There were old-fashioned saloon doors and a map of the area paint-ed on the wall behind a giant pool table. I turned to Dad, hoping he'd gotten what he wanted from the view. We got back in our cars.

The streets were silent as we made the final drive to my new home. Some of them were concrete but many were dirt. Charmingly bright-coloured cottages sat beside small industrial mining build-ings fashioned from shipping containers that were surrounded by chain-link fences. From what I could see, these were the only two types of buildings in Wells. There was no plastic McDonald's, no concrete establishments for banks or offices, no suburban homes made of brick or stone.

The staff house was a small, one-storey white cottage surrounded by gravel. On one side of the exterior was a big mural depicting rab-bits running impressionistically in a circle.

Dad and I approached and knocked quietly, unsure if anyone would be home. Finding the door unlocked, we entered cautiously, encountering a short set of stairs, which we tiptoed up. Inside, a tall, thin girl of about thirty-two with a diamond-shaped face and wavy auburn hair sat in the kitchen, apparently waiting for us. She turned out to be my roommate, Hannah, the archivist of Barkerville. She stood from her chair and smiled without opening her lips. Her nose was round, and she had a few visibly grey strands in her hair.

"Hi," she said.

"Hi," I replied in a voice that didn't feel like my own, self-conscious about interacting with someone in front of my father.

"Welcome to your new home," she said ceremoniously. She looked around, aware of my seeing the space for the first time.

Dad slipped out, whispering about grabbing my bags. I felt spoiled for taking him with me all the way from Ontario, that I didn't have to get my bags from the car because he wanted to do it for me.

An orange cat ran into the kitchen.

"Aren't you the sweetest!" I said, crouching down. The cat approached me, and I stretched out my hand. I love cats, and had missed them. My roommates in England didn't have any pets, and most apartments had rules against them. The cat rubbed against my hand and flopped to one side.

"I'm going to put you in a pie!" I said to the cat. I looked up at Hannah and wondered if she would be happy to see me touching her cat, or if she was someone who was competitive about pets.

"I think someone's looking to open up a Chinese restaurant — better watch out, Lily!" she said to the cat. Hannah smiled a toothy smile, and I saw that her face expanded very wide when she did so, and there was a sharpness to it. It reminded me of the Cheshire Cat.

It had been a long time since I had heard something so unambiguously racist. I said nothing, in hopes that she might interpret my silence as unalienating disapproval. *Coward*, I thought of myself. I stood up.

Dad set my bags in the kitchen.

"Well, Jelly Bean, I think it's time for me to let you get settled." Dad was like this even on the phone. Always efficient, probably harbouring some secret timeline he wanted to stick to but not at the cost of his friendliness.

He gave me a brief hug and said goodbye to Hannah. I watched him out the window as he got in the rental car to return to Prince George. I turned back to Hannah, whose face had contracted back to her closed mouth smirk that I couldn't interpret. I felt spoiled again. I had gotten exactly what I had wanted: for Dad to come but only to help me with the essential things, and then to disappear so I could begin integrating into my new life. Hannah had seen this, and I was ashamed.

I had two bedrooms to choose from, one at the end of the hall with a double bed and a smaller one toward the living room and across from the bathroom with a single bed. I chose the double, which was also across from Hannah's room. The room had empty off-white walls, and the bed frame had no headboard. There was a closet, a small dresser, and a bedside table.

I took in the room. For a minute I let myself off the hook for decorating, but then reminded myself that six months is actually a very long time and would not pass quickly, and I would be happier if I maybe put up some small decorations.

I had a bad habit of perceiving temporary stays, like my year in England, as short, and so I always forgot to do many of the things that made spaces more comfortable, like investing in new items that I might have to leave behind or painting the walls a colour I liked. Instead, I'd treat these transient homes like liminal spaces between my childhood and some adult person who I would eventually become, though I wasn't sure when. I had learned about liminal spaces in England, as they were a popular topic of study for medieval archaeologists. Liminal spaces are places of transition, like entranceways to churches that a holy man might cross through during a religious ceremony, or rooms between the kitchens and the great halls in a late medieval manor house, where different people had a different type of access based on their status. You were only there for a moment, but they were also functional and meaningful in an intangible way — unnoticed and highly important.

I had once tried to explain my relationship with these temporary living spaces to a friend because it seemed to me like a real problem in my life, but she had told me that many people felt this way and this was not a unique problem, and to stop dwelling on it. I vowed to promptly unpack in the staff house room and leave my mark on the space, however temporary it would be.

Hannah said all the cookware and dishes were hers. I would later learn this was not true and that Hannah was lying or had perhaps forgotten. She told me she had lived in the house for four years and had seen many temporary interns, summer students, and contract workers come and go. This made sense: the house was tidy but cluttered, as if hundreds of people had each left two or three small items here. In one corner was an open piano, with sheet music strewn haphazardly on the seat.

"It's a bit sad saying goodbye to people so much," she said. Hannah had a small stutter, and this made her repeat words sometimes. "People come and go so much here, it's hard to form attachments only to say goodbye," she continued, somewhat accusingly, as if I had taken this job only to become attached to her and say goodbye, and maybe I should have considered that before accepting the position.

She asked me how old I was.

"Twenty-four."

"Oh, I was thinking you were more like twenty."

"People sometimes say I seem younger than I am."

"Me, too," she said, and smiled with teeth again.

"Oh, how old are you?" I asked. Observing her, I thought she might be in her thirties, or at youngest, her late twenties.

"Twenty-six."

"Oh."

I was tired and wanted to go to sleep in my new bed without unpacking, but it felt nonsensical and lame to be the type of person who takes an obscure and strange job in the mountains, but is uncurious about the surroundings. So instead, I let Hannah drive me to Barkerville in her blue hatchback.

The drive was about ten minutes on a winding road with a speed limit of forty. Hannah, used to the route, drove seventy. The road to Barkerville was charming and unspoiled by human activity except for a small, dark wood cabin we passed at one point, which was surrounded by nautical decorations and a sign that read "Kemptville." Hannah explained that the man who lived there was a long-time resident who, years ago, had abandoned "downtown" Wells to live in isolation, just one kilometre from his previous home across from the Wells Hotel, after a long-standing disagreement with the other townspeople. His last name was Kempt, Hannah explained.

"What didn't they agree on?" I asked.

"Oh, you know," said Hannah, and she stopped speaking as if she suddenly didn't care. I gazed out at the marshland full of Christmas trees of many breeds, some spindly with grey trunks and some with robust brown ones. What I liked best were the clouds, which hung low in the sky and intermingled with the fir trees due to the altitude. The clouds were behaving normally, it was us who insisted on coming up so high.

Nearing Barkerville, we approached a large red-painted wooden sign that read "Barkerville Historic Town & Park" beside an image of an old bearded man. I recognized this man as Billy Barker. I'd learned through my research that Billy had not been a particularly special man, but he'd been a successful miner for a very short period in 1861 when the town was founded, and so it was named after him. He died, broke and alone, only a few years later and was buried in a pauper's grave. Prospecting in the nineteenth-century gold rush, it seemed, was a lot like gambling, except if you didn't win big you were stuck in the middle of the mountains with a few provisions and only one pair of muddy shoes.

Shoes were especially valuable in nineteenth-century Barkerville because they were so expensive, and a bad pair of shoes would leave you with fungus and you might need to get your foot sawn off to save you. People slept in their boots, and sometimes people would try to pry them from your feet as you did so. Laundresses made their fortunes cleaning men's stinking socks. I thought of Samson and Delilah, and Delilah stealing Samson's shoes and leaving him helpless in his remote mine instead of cutting off his hair.

Barkerville had two narrow streets running parallel to one another: a main street and a back street, which the staff used when they didn't want to be seen by tourists. By this time of year, the park's open season was just about over, and there weren't any tourists anyway. I stood in the parking lot and peered up the main street, which was built on a slight incline, so you could see the entire stretch of road from the entrance. The streets were lined with old wooden buildings — it looked like the sets of the Westerns I used to watch. At the end of the street was Chinatown, where none of the buildings were painted, and all the signs were red with vertical gold lettering.

I could see tiny, costumed people travelling up and down the street in the distance. The women wore giant, floor-length dresses in bright colours, and the men wore muted plain clothes and leather hats.

The altitude in Barkerville was even higher than in Wells, and the air was much cooler. I tried to feel for some difference or thinness in the air, but detected none beyond the temperature.

Hannah went into the administrative building by herself, saying she had some "archive business" to attend to. Before she left, she told me to tell the attendants in the visitors' centre that I was the new intern so that they would let me in for free.

In the visitors' centre I met Brandon, an attendant sitting behind a long desk beside a woman in her fifties with a deep V-neck
and long dyed hair with straight bangs. He was about my age
and was very tall, with a scruffy beard and and coarse brown hair
that stuck out from under his toque. His perfectly circular glasses
magnified his eyes. He was wearing a red vest with the Barkerville
logo on the breast. I told him I was the new intern and we shook
hands. I yawned.

Observing this, Brandon told me that the elevation in Wells and
Barkerville was just at the point where it began to really affect the
body. Like the old man by my locked car, Brandon, too, was eager
to fill me in on the minute aspects of life in Barkerville. His speech
was polished and concise, suggesting he'd said this many times before to other newcomers and visitors alike.

"That's probably why you're so tired," he said.

"Oh," I said, and nodded. I wondered what exactly being affect-
ed by altitude consisted of. Could you die? Should I have known
about this?

"You'll adjust in a few days," he continued, "but you'll sleep well
tonight. Don't drink any alcohol though, you'll get super drunk."
He said this as if he were really excited about how deeply I would
sleep and how drunk I would get.

"I won't, thanks," I said. "It was nice to meet you. I'm going to
go see the town now."

"See you around," he said. "I'll show you Wells later this week
if you want."

"That would be nice," I said. "Goodbye." I waved with two
hands like a mime and went out through the large glass doors.

Barkerville was exciting. I had seen many photos, but I hadn't
anticipated the way it would feel to be inside. I thought it might be
like visiting the cabin at Walden Pond, or when you played with
Lego as a kid and the buildings were disproportionate and sparse

compared to the humans or Lego people. But Barkerville was dense, with big, detailed buildings close to one another, and the road was muddy, which made you feel like it actually was the miserable nineteenth century.

I was shy around the interpreters in the streets and inside some buildings I entered, standing at their assigned positions like Westworld robots but sometimes clustered together in conversation with one another when I was far away. I could not initiate conversation, but when they addressed me I revealed myself as the new archival intern for the winter. I found that I spoke as if it was some sort of ironic joke, and I was trying to vocalize air quotes around my new title.

The blacksmith, who was handsome and had an impressive head of grey hair, said that I had big bags under my eyes. "You know, Barkerville is at just the right altitude to start affecting the body," he said serenely.

• • •

That evening, soft snowflakes fell from the sky and dusted the grass. I looked out my window; it was all beautiful and peaceful, even the industrial building a few yards away. I felt tucked away somehow, and that I did not need to account for my whereabouts on social media. I fell asleep quickly and slept soundly, dreaming of gliding through the forest.

Chapter 2

THE NEXT MORNING THE SNOW WAS REPLACED WITH A LOW mist that hung between the trees longer and closer to me than I thought it possibly could. I got up and put on my overalls, which were hyperfeminine — they had no buckles, and had little flowers embroidered all over them that dug into my skin if I sat in them for too long.

In the kitchen, I made myself eggs for breakfast. I asked Hannah if I could use her pans and salt and pepper.

"What else would you use?" Hannah said.

"I'd cook them right on the burner, of course," I joked.

"Um, okay?" Hannah said, widening her eyes and looking around as if searching for another spectator to identify with.

I scrambled my eggs and ate them with a piece of toast. I'd forgotten to buy butter, but thought better of asking Hannah for some of hers.

On the fridge were a Princess Leia magnet that read "A Woman's Place Is in the Resistance," a wedding invitation featuring a cartoon fox, and a sticker that just said "bitch." On the wall above the kitchen table was a framed drawing of a naked woman flying to the moon.

The cat came into the kitchen and approached me, rubbing against the legs of the chair. I reached my hand down and scratched her arching back.

"Hi, Lily!" I said. Hannah told me her full name was Tiger Lily.

"Like Peter Pan," she said proudly.

"Oh, yeah," I said. I wondered if Hannah had trouble avoiding saying racist things but only in matters related to her cat.

Tiger Lily changed her mind about being petted, and she swiped at my hand, leaving a scratch, and ran out of the room. I grinned sheepishly at Hannah, who was now in the doorway and had seen the whole sorry encounter. I didn't want her to think I took the scratch personally, even though it was starting to bleed. Hannah laughed, like she had caught me in a lie.

"That's the thing about cats. They *know* they're assholes, but we love them anyway. Don't we, Lily?"

"I don't really think cats are assholes," I said. "I feel like they're probably just setting boundaries."

"Okay …" said Hannah, her eyes widening again. I now wondered if she was resistant to the idea that Lily wasn't an asshole, and that's why she kept saying racist things around her.

"I guess what I mean is, people often say they like cats because they're assholes, and sure they can be assholes, but I think we actually like them because they're sweet and cute, and we wouldn't really like a cat if it was only an asshole. And I don't think Lily is an asshole."

Hannah laughed incredulously. "Well, I never thought about it *that* much."

I hadn't planned any activities beyond breakfast. I was still so surprised to be in Wells at all. I looked out the window. Then I opened my computer, and saw that Brandon had found me on social media and had sent me a message only a few minutes before.

"Hi Josie, it's Brandon from Barkerville. Do you want to go on a little stroll this morning?"

I typed my reply: "Hi Brandon, sure! :))))"

I met Brandon behind the Jack O' Clubs, in the parking lot where the gas pumps were. He was fifteen minutes late, and I was five minutes early, even though it was so cold out that I'd had to turn back to grab my toque, which had a conspicuous pompom on top that weighed more than the entire rest of the hat, so it flopped around when I walked. The gas pumps were really old. Something I noticed about Wells was that many things were old-fashioned, and it was impossible to tell if they were that way on purpose, or simply the result of the passage of time. Surely someone in a different place would have thought to replace these ancient gas pumps, which I later learned could only be turned on from inside the station by the attendant, making the process of pumping gas at least three minutes longer than it needed to be.

Brandon smelled like smoke when he arrived. It wasn't a vague or subtle smell; it was deeply set into his clothes and his beard, seeping out and wafting toward me in waves. I wasn't sure if this nauseated or intrigued me. As he approached, I became aware of how much taller he was than me. His smell and his height made me feel like an eighth grader going to do drugs with some sophomores behind the gym in a coming-of-age movie. When he smiled toothily at me, I reminded myself that I had just made that story up. He beamed down at me, larger than life from behind his glasses.

"Hello," I said. "Thank you for inviting me." I realized I was nervous, because I was shifting my weight on my feet very quickly. It struck me that this walk with Brandon was the first thing I'd chosen to do myself in my new home. Had I made the right decision? Brandon took off confidently, implying that I should follow him.

He led me past the gas pumps and into the marshy bush behind us. There was a dirt walking path and tan-coloured reeds and tall grass that closed behind us as we went by.

I was saying lots of nice and general things: "Nice day for it!" "Sure is like *Westworld*, here, huh? 'Not much of a rind on you!'" I talked a lot, but I wasn't saying much of anything. When I reminded myself to stop, I found my jaw was tired.

Brandon was patient as I said all of these nonsense nothings. Once I stopped, he took a breath and began to tell me about himself. He was a painter from Medicine Hat.

"I was born in Calgary, though," he added, pronouncing it Cal-Gree. He had gone to university in Montreal, just like me. Because he was six years older than I was, we never lived there at the same time. He left right before I arrived, and he ended up doing a bunch of residencies and internships at Island Mountain Arts, the local arts organization, which is how he ended up in Wells permanently.

"I just fell in love with it here. It's like how someone completely different from you can become your best friend," he said.

We discussed our favourite locations in Montreal, but we found that we had not heard of any of the same places. We shrugged and instead focused on the general features of the city that we both liked and were generally popular: buying booze in corner stores and being legally allowed to drink it at the park, the European nature of the architecture and the culture, and the diverse and inexpensive food options.

"Montreal just has this incredible energy, where you can just be outside, having a smoke, and just meet the most amazing person, you know?" said Brandon.

I nodded, but I didn't really know.

It turned out he was talking about only one person, his ex-girlfriend, who he'd met outside of a noise show at a bar downtown. Based on what I knew of Brandon already, I thought this meeting probably had more to do with the fact that he was a very extroverted person, and maybe the fact that they were both smokers, than their being in Montreal.

He said he was so poor when he was in Montreal that he once subsisted on only an enormous sack of potatoes for an entire month. I could not imagine what that was like, and was self-conscious about trying to make the right face in response.

Now, he was between jobs but was applying for a marketing and digital media position in Barkerville.

"I hope you get it." I said.

"Thank you," he said. We grinned at each other. It's so easy to be friends with someone. You just have to tell them you hope good things happen to them.

In the marsh, he took me to the delta of two streams.

"This is 'the Y,'" he said, and chuckled to himself. "We call it 'the Y intersection.'" This didn't mean anything to me, but I smiled, and he did, too.

"In the summer, people who come to work here sometimes have to work out of their cars, and they wash their clothes here, and swim."

I dipped my hand in. It was icy cold.

"Well, it's too cold to swim in now, obviously, unless you're a daredevil," said Brandon.

We headed toward town. As we did so, Brandon told me the various names of the mountains. They were not "big" mountains like the Rockies, all covered in stone, but were instead coated by trees with small rocky peaks at the top. In Wells there was Slide Mountain, which appeared to "slide" as you moved through town and could be seen clearly from many different places. There was also Cow Mountain, and Bald Mountain, and the Two Sisters Mountains.

When we found our way back to town, I noticed there were paintings on a lot of the buildings, like the one of rabbits on the staff house.

Brandon explained that these paintings were part of an annual auction where artists offer their paintings to be displayed on the home of the highest bidder. It kept the town kooky.

The best painting was of Fred Wells, the town's founder, who looked a bit like Arthur the aardvark, his giant, larger-than-life head peeking over the horizon and looking out onto the town like God. The painting was yellow, evoking an apocalyptic atmosphere, as if Fred Wells was Ozymandias looking over his empire.

Brandon kept talking to me and telling me stuff about his life, but I became awkward and stilted in town. It was so quiet and flat, and Brandon's voice, which was kind of grumbly, seemed to carry so far it bounced off of the distant mountains before returning to us again. Maybe he noticed that I was nervous, because he turned to me and said, "I will say, the trees have ears here."

"Oh?"

"Definitely. Everyone knows your business, so be careful what you say." He raised his eyebrows playfully. I nodded solemnly, even though the idea of someone being interested in my private life was thrilling to me.

As it happened, Brandon had not planned a simple walk through the town. He told me he had something awesome to show me, and he led me down a smaller dirt road, away from town.

"You're going to love this," he said.

"Is it a World War II fighter jet?" I asked.

"No?"

We walked for about ten minutes, and I wondered if he was going to murder me. He was a few paces in front of me. I studied the back of his head, and the backside of his coat, and his butt. He seemed too jolly to be a murderer.

Eventually, he stopped. It was unclear why at first, but he gestured to a building that was partially hidden by the thick brush of flora.

Brandon was right. It was pretty cool. The structure was hexagonal, or maybe octagonal, homemade of wood tiles, like a strange little castle. It was obviously abandoned, but still appeared to be fairly new. There were construction materials littered carelessly beside it.

"A couple from Vancouver moved here and built this, but they had to move back to the city for some reason before they could finish," Brandon explained. "Good riddance."

He wanted to go inside. He said he'd done it a ton before, and it was really cool because the ceilings were weird and geometric. I was trying to listen, but I was starting to feel separated from myself, like I was watching us talk on a TV, and I just wanted to turn it off and go to bed.

"Huh," I said, "sure." But I didn't follow him when he moved toward the house. There were rusty nails on the stairs, and all of sudden I was the eighth grader with a sophomore again.

"Do you not wanna go?" he asked. I shrugged and started toward the house until I slipped on a patch of mud and fell on my ass.

"Oh shit!" said Brandon.

"I don't think I want to go in there," I said. I was awash with embarrassment, having been revealed to be, at heart, an unadventurous person. Brandon looked down at me kindly anyway.

He moved to help me up, but I scrambled to my feet without him, holding a hand out, imploring him to stay away. I did not like the idea of being touched just then.

Instead of going into the house, Brandon said he'd take me to the Wells Hotel Pub. I peeked behind me to check my butt; there was lots of mud.

"It's not that bad," he said. I pulled a twig from my hair. Brandon was unaffected by this roadblock. He took all of this in stride and was going on as if everything was the same, even though I thought I was behaving needlessly grumpily.

In the pub, Brandon moved directly to the bar, where a woman with thick curly hair and an exciting, elaborately coloured knit sweater was sitting, nursing a bowl of soup, chatting with a friendly looking man sitting beside her. Brandon greeted the woman. She had sleepy eyelids; she hazily looked in my direction. Brandon sat down beside her, and after a minute, so did I, on his other side. The woman slid a hand across Brandon toward me.

"I'm Sharon," she said.

"Josie."

The bartender emerged from the back room. He was cute, and he and Brandon exchanged private looks with one another, which were then directed, briefly, toward me. I could tell they must've been friends.

"So, what do you like to do in your free time, Josie?" asked Sharon.

"I don't have any hobbies because I'm such a deep thinker," I said. "Just kidding. Um, sometimes I write poetry." I was referring to the two poems I had written at 2:00 a.m. three weeks previously, when I was feeling emotional about something that I couldn't remember in the morning.

Sharon told me that she was the Presentation and Preservation Director at Barkerville. She was responsible for overseeing all interpretation and the archives and curatorial department.

"So, you could say I'm your boss, Nancy's boss."

Sharon was married to Ricky, the man sitting on her other side. He was engaged in lively conversation with some scraggly looking people.

I wanted to go back to the staff house. I was still jet lagged, and my butt was starting to get sore. But I didn't want to leave Brandon alone, lest he tell everyone the story of how I ate shit in front of the geometric house. I had the same soup that Sharon did, and I learned that the bartender's name was Henrick.

Sharon asked me lots of questions about myself and my decision to move to Wells, which was nice, even though I didn't have good answers. I didn't think what I had done was all that odd, and after all, hadn't Barkerville expected someone to move there for the job? It felt less brave than moving back in with my parents, or going back to Montreal and trying to reintegrate with my old classmates. Wouldn't anyone feel that way? Wouldn't Sharon?

On the way home, the whole conversation and the entire first half of my day started to feel terribly wrong. I spent the rest of the afternoon in bed, alternating between naps and Netflix.

That night was Wells's "Annual Chili Cook-Off." It was a benefit for the fire department, and the winner took home a grand prize. Hannah said that someone called Lyle Smith would certainly take the prize, as he always did. Each year, his chili contained lots of different types of meat, like moose, caribou, and deer.

"If the same people enter year after year, do they have to invent a new chili recipe?" I asked Hannah, who smiled and said nothing.

On top of being the Barkerville archivist, Hannah was the fire chief in Wells. She showed me her walkie-talkie and her pager, which she kept on the coffee table when she was home, or strapped to her waist when she was out. If there was a fire, the pager emitted a loud sound to propel her into action. She told me she always had to be on call, and when she drove to Quesnel to do errands, the deputy had to know, so that he could be on call instead.

For the event, she made a batch of southern-style biscuits, which took up half the fridge. She had to go in early to help set up, and I helped her carry over the biscuits.

Entry was $5. The Wells Community Hall featured an enormous open floor with a ceiling three stories high and steps flanking either side to sit on. It reminded me of the dance hall in *It's a Wonderful Life*. The room was huge, with little stations set up at tables spaced out evenly throughout the room. At each table was a crock pot or large container of chili and the responsible chef.

There were many people in the hall, but it felt empty due to its size. I saw, in the distance, the man with the cigarette from the day before. He was engaged in bright conversation with a woman with a limp ponytail and a polar fleece sweater.

The people in Wells seemed to be mostly older than me. There were many women in their forties, and a few proud, middle-aged couples with their hands on the smalls of each other's backs. I spotted Brandon at the far end of the hall with Henrick and a group of boys around my age. He saw me and waved, a friendly expression on his face, but did not break his conversation.

Hannah introduced me to Jeremy, the fire deputy. He was handsome in a remarkable way, like a movie star. He had a ruddy face, speckled with something like rosacea, a patchy beard, and startlingly clean, shiny reddish hair. He was attractive in a way that tricks you into thinking he was just really, really regular looking, and everyone else around him was just sick or old. He told me that he was also an interpreter.

Hannah explained that Jeremy's eyebrows and beard were a little bit patchy because on Victoria Day that year, as he was lighting a fireworks display at Barkerville, they'd ignited in his face and singed off much of his hair and burned his face, which was why he appeared sunburned.

We stood in the hall en masse, excitedly holding our paper plates in anticipation of an inexpensive dinner.

There were twelve chilis in total, and it took a long time to walk between them. Hannah joined me, and we both scooped a tiny ladle of chili onto our plates at each station. We used chips, cornbread, and biscuits to separate the entries from one another.

Lyle Smith's chili certainly did have all the advertised wild meats, and whispers around the room suggested that there might be even more, like whistle pig or bear. I recognized Lyle — he was an interpreter I'd seen at the printing press in Barkerville the day before. He was a trim, elderly man with sunken eyes like a Dickensian villain. His chili sat proudly before him in a large vat that smelled curious and titillating.

I had no interest in trying new meats. I was introduced to meat as a child, before I understood that I was eating the flesh of a living thing. The unfamiliarity of the taste of a new meat as an adult makes me painfully aware of the facts of life, while my childhood meats just feel like food in my mouth.

Many of the chilis had diverse meats like Lyle Smith's. I could not decide whether to prioritize avoiding these tables or sticking close to Hannah. In the end I did neither well, and ended up wandering aimlessly, taking only a few types of chili so as to appear randomly discerning rather than prejudiced against moose.

I was surprised by the innovation demonstrated by the various entries. Each smelled different from the last. One chili had corn, and the aroma made my eyes well up. One was more beige than brown or red, with little green bits sitting in it. Some were gross. The contestants stood proudly or shyly by their pots.

Hannah and I sat down at the tables, her plate piled a little higher than mine because of my pickiness. I realized I was gearing up to defend myself. Hannah did not ask, but she did raise her eyebrows.

Around us, the guests sat down, some at our table. A woman I had seen earlier in the visitors' centre plunked down beside us. She introduced herself as Veronica.

"I'm Josie," I said.

"So, we've got you for the winter?"

"Looks like it."

"Hannah told me your daddy came to drop you off all the way from Ontario!" This felt both intensely confrontational and sincerely friendly. It was as if she thought, based on my appearance, that I might like to hear this. I wondered if anyone would like to hear this, and if this was a reasonable assumption to make about me. I was glad I had changed out of my girlish overalls before the event.

I didn't respond to her question about my "daddy" because she kept speaking.

"Lots of people come for the summer, but not many for the winter. We're just winding down this year; people are leaving this week and won't be back again till May. You're going to be pretty lonely all the way out here." Her expression suddenly changed and she flashed her eyes at me as if to scold me, like she was angry with me for being so irresponsible.

"Maybe that's true!" I said. I had lived in a few different places in my life and had been lonely in some of them. But loneliness felt random, as if geography or demographics had little to do with it. Veronica sighed as if it was useless to reason with me.

Murmurs passed through the crowd as more people entered the hall. Two interpreters named Greg Chapman and Josh Mitchell had met a black bear in their front yard in the afternoon. The bear had broken into the toolshed, and it didn't see them when they came outside because it was still rifling around inside, and they ran back into the house and avoided being mauled. Hannah told me that bears didn't come into Wells very often, but it was happening more frequently because tourists were getting out of their cars to look at them and sometimes threw them food. They'd become unafraid of humans.

"People think they can just get out of their cars and approach a bear, a wild animal," said Hannah, rolling her eyes. I made a note that, to avoid having Hannah ever roll her eyes at me, I should not ever approach a bear.

My favourite chili was the ugly grey one with the green bits, which turned out to be green pepper. I ranked it first on a little piece of paper, and ranked Lyle Smith's third because everyone spoke so highly of it. Lyle Smith won, and was given a pint glass with the fire department logo on it, which he held high above his head victoriously.

• • •

The next day was my first day of work. Hannah woke up only twenty minutes before nine, and, carrying a carton of half and half for her coffee, was groggy on the drive to Barkerville. The drive was beautiful. As we drove toward the rising sun, there were intriguing shadows, cast by the new position of the sun, that made the trip new again to me, as if I hadn't been there only the day before.

In the administrative building I met my boss, Nancy, in her office, which I recognized from my Skype interview. I sat in the chair she had moved in front of her desk for me specifically.

Nancy had big watery eyes like a cartoon bunny and intimidating, smart glasses with hot pink rims. She was kind but didn't smile often. It occurred to me that I always expected women to smile at me a lot, because women want to make each other feel good. At that time I believed that that was what makes us different from men, who don't often think about how others feel in any given situation. I made an effort to mirror Nancy by smiling less.

She asked what I wanted to accomplish during my internship.

"Ummm ..." I wasn't expecting this question. Wasn't it obvious that I was happy to have any job in a museum? I would have peeled potatoes so long as I could call myself a curatorial intern and put it on my resumé.

At McGill University, I had known many people who would have had wonderful answers to this question. My peers were the types of people to have ideas about how to change the world, and to actually think they were worth executing. They were also wealthy in a way I wasn't. Not that I was hard done by, but their dreams materialized with a phone call to a relative.

In my final semester I directed a stage adaptation of the graphic novel *Ghost World*. All of the student reporters for their respective student newspapers, who were no doubt very passionate about their mission as truth-tellers, asked me: Why *Ghost World*? What was so urgent about directing this play?

The truth was that I had wanted to direct a play because it sounded fun, and I liked *Ghost World*, and I knew people would come see it because it was a well-known graphic novel, and lots of people knew it because of the movie. I don't think it mattered at all to anyone other than me whether or not the play happened. I told the student reporters that I was interested in intertextuality and theories of adaptation. They nodded seriously and printed that in the papers.

Nancy continued. "Our previous intern, Sita, was fascinated by historical clothing, and she spent a lot of time cataloguing and archiving items of clothing and sewing patterns, things like that. She created a project about it at the end." I felt mad at Sita for this. Weren't interns meant to watch out for each other by not making each other look bad?

"Ummm ... that's a great question," I said. "Well, I suppose I'm mostly just interested in learning about Barkerville in general, and helping where I can — Oh! And grant writing! I want to learn about grant writing!" This was not a lie. I remembered that lots of non-profits and arts organizations needed to apply for grants to secure funding for projects, and that grant writing was difficult, and that you had to do it many times before you could really put it on your resumé.

Nancy told me that they apply for all sorts of grants all the time, and that there would certainly be an opportunity for me to help in preparing them.

She showed me how to enter the names and descriptions of archival photos from the physical catalogue into the digital catalogue on the computer. I sat at the big table in the centre of the room, while Hannah sat in an open nook that was also her office. I flipped through binders of photos all day, and gazed at the faces of the nineteenth and twentieth century inhabitants of Barkerville and Wells, or giant pits where men mined, or heritage interpreters from the seventies.

As I did so, I remembered my undergraduate class "Poetics of the Image," which was about interpreting movies and photographs. Our professor, a pale woman with a harsh New York accent, explained to us that the *punctum* is the part of an image that sticks with you, or "pierces" you in a poignant way. She said that the punctum is objective and not debatable, and that every picture ever taken has one.

"No," she had said of a Victorian photograph of a family posing with a deceased child. "The punctum is not this woman's wry smile, but her bracelet." I didn't understand why it was so clear that the punctum was the bracelet and not the smile, but I wrote it down anyway.

Later, a friend of mine who hated this professor told me she had been wrong, and that the punctum was obviously subjective because Roland Barthes had said so, and that she was probably just being a bitch.

I picked a punctum in each photograph in the archive: a blurry horse turning his head to see something. An arm cocked just so. A gun. A beagle, looking forlorn and unloved in the mud. A lot of my punctums were animals.

Many of the people in the photos were unattractive. They had faces that didn't make sense and mean expressions, even the prosperous people who built fine houses and had many healthy children. I wondered if only unattractive people had the inclination to go into mining and move to the Cariboo region, and if my being in the Cariboo made me unattractive by default. In my brain, I knew that was both insane and an overly simplistic way of thinking about the world, and unfair to the miners in the nineteenth century, not to mention to myself.

I was becoming aware of the fact that I spent much of my inner life fighting these taxonomies that suddenly occurred to me, and battling my depressing placements within them. When I was having a lovely day I would often be struck by a thought like: "What if all women who dye their hair unnaturally blond are considered desperate?" or "What if people with student debt have a harder time in love than those who have no student debt, and I have ruined my love life forever?" I was beginning to suspect that I moved unpredictably through the world in order to avoid these categorizations that at times seemed to certainly exist.

Brandon came into the archives and said hello to me and Hannah.

"I was wondering if either of you wanted to come to a show tonight. There's a band at the Jack O' Clubs."

Hannah hardly glanced up when she said no, thank you, but I said yes. I thought maybe Brandon and I were going to become friends, which excited me because I didn't find him attractive in any way. My friend Lara, years before, had told me that I had an unusual way of thinking about men. She said that most women thought that men were always trying to sleep with them and falling in love with them, while I was always afraid they thought that's what I was doing. Since then I'd been trying to see things the way I was supposed to, like I could destroy a man very easily with my wiles, but it all just seemed a little far-fetched to me.

"Be careful," said Hannah from her nook when Brandon left.

"What do you mean?"

"Brandon sleeps with everyone," Hannah explained, still not meeting my eyes, and instead focusing on an archival photograph with intent, as if she was performing her blocking in a sitcom. "He'll probably try to sleep with you. He slept with the last girl who lived in the house even though she told me she wasn't going to."

"Oh," I said, blinking. I didn't know anything about men.

Another job I was expected to perform, which Nancy outlined, was cataloguing donations to Barkerville's permanent collection of artifacts. These could be directly related to Barkerville's history, or only tangentially connected. For example, we received a red velvet Fez that was once part of the uniform of the fire department in Wells, for some reason. We also received a large deposit of unused women's underwear from the 1960s, safe in their packaging, which featured a drawing of a woman performing calisthenics. We also received a multitude of glass bottles. I was to learn that glass bottles were the most popular type of artifact donation. In the coming weeks Hannah would take me to the storage facility that housed thousands of glass bottles, sitting side by side on shelf after shelf, too boring to make use of but too authentically historical to throw away.

As time went on, I would come to find that I did not like depositing artifacts in the storage facilities, most of which were inside unused historic buildings, or in the attics around town. Many of these spaces did not have light fixtures, and so we had to feel our way around using flashlights. It was at these times that I'd wonder if I would meet any of the ghosts who might have lived in Barkerville.

Whenever I'd ask the security guards about supernatural activity, they would only offer either remarkably anti-superstitious responses, or exaggerated tales of Barkervillian horror that would make me feel stupid for asking. In truth, for a place with so many suicides, there were few legends.

The worst place would prove to be the attic of the Nichol Hotel Museum, where Barkerville had decided to store all of the most horrible artifacts, including broken clocks, Victorian dolls, and historic dentures of ambiguous make — long wrenched from the mouths of their toothless owners.

At the end of the day, I met Brandon at the Jack O' Clubs, arriving early again. Inside, its three stories were all hollowed out and had a vaguely Ancient Egyptian theme. There were stylized hieroglyphics on the walls, and a great winged woman above the stage.

This decor was left over from when the Jack O' Clubs was a casino during the 1930s, styled in as Art Nouveau a way as possible for a remote mountain town. The interior had evidently been altered as time passed. There were booths that must have been from the 1990s, and modern light fixtures, and an ambiguously coloured carpet that could have indicated any time period at all. The Egyptian decor mingled with more Wild West motifs and decorations. The room reminded me of the ship of Theseus, and made me wonder how long it would take before all of the original materials to make the building were gone and lost to time.

Attached to the Jack's main room was an annex that functioned as a general store, where they sold expensive food (a jar of tomato sauce was $18), cigarettes, hunting equipment, and souvenirs. This was also where the town's Canada Post office operated, and also where you could buy gas from the old-fashioned pumps outside.

That night the big room was mostly empty. There was a beautiful young woman behind the bar, and a few men sitting at tables, alone or in pairs, not speaking, or speaking so quietly I could not tell. They were mostly white men, wearing flannel or windbreakers, looking like the type of boys who played hockey in my hometown. Their faces were diverse in age but all severe and unwelcoming. They stared into their pints with concentration and determination. On the stage, the band, three long-haired boys in T-shirts, were setting up their instruments and amps. The noises they made seemed to disturb the patrons, whose eyes kept flickering quickly to the stage, their brows furrowed, and quickly back again.

When Brandon arrived, smelling just as strongly of smoke as the previous day, he explained that the Jack was popular with the miners, who mostly kept to themselves, while the hotel pub was the choice of most locals.

"And never the twain shall meet," I said, gesturing dramatically with my hands. Brandon responded with a noise that sounded halfway between "huh" and "hah." I investigated Brandon's face and his clothes and his mannerisms closely for clues about whether or not Hannah was right that Brandon was trying to sleep with me, but this made me feel overstimulated and itchy.

I was wearing lipstick with mascara but no eyeliner, and a sleeveless turtleneck with pants that I considered to be completely unremarkable. I couldn't tell if this was a normal thing to wear, or if it was slutty. I found I had no information about the situation no matter how much I analyzed, apart from what Hannah had told me.

My older sister, Maddie, was always making statements about men and what they liked and what they didn't like when we were teenagers. She would say, "Josie, men do not like women who have tiny thin lips like mine. You will be popular with men because you have nice full lips." And yet, I was always seeing women with tiny thin lips walking around and holding hands with their boyfriends, and I never had a boyfriend. Meanwhile, Maddie, with her tiny thin lips, had had many boyfriends. I suspected what was happening was that Maddie was popular with men for some elusive reason that neither she nor I could name, and this gave her confident but incorrect insights into how men thought, and what they wanted. They wanted her, but she probably didn't actually know what made her lovable, just like I didn't know what made me so unlovable.

Slowly, the Jack accumulated a small audience of about fifteen for the concert, including an elderly couple and a few miners who chose to remain for the show, and simply turned in their seats to watch the stage. About six of the audience members were Brandon's friends, most of whom I recognized as interpreters I'd seen at Barkerville on my visit the day before. They were the young men in Barkerville's courthouse, and a few from the street, all in their early to mid-twenties. Henrick was there, still handsome, and one of the boys wore a poncho and a wide-brimmed hat that annoyed me.

The boys formed a little group on the other side of the room, and did not approach Brandon and me but gestured hello to him. His friend in the poncho fixed his eyes on me, moving them up and down. He and Brandon looked at each other, and his friend nodded and smiled. Watching this happen in real time made me feel like a slutty character in a teen sex movie. I was just then struck by a strong sense of solidarity with slutty teen sex movie characters.

It was frustrating to be sexually assessed by a man in a poncho.

Instead of bringing me over to his friends, Brandon told me to wait where I was while he said hello to them. I went to the bathroom and wiped off my lipstick.

When I came back, the band was playing loud punk music. As I entered the bar room, it was as though the eyes of every man slowly turned toward me. The drummer, in the throes of his craft, even smiled at me. The ponchoed man glanced over at Brandon, who had returned to my side, once again. I had a terrible feeling that I shouldn't have left them alone. To me, there is nothing scarier than when men discuss a woman when there are no other women around.

That evening, I couldn't sleep. I got out of bed, and I took a pair of scissors from the kitchen to the bathroom and cut my long blond hair to just below my chin.

"Ummm ... are you ok?" Hannah, still up, asked when I came out of the bathroom, looking slightly afraid at my drastic transformation.

"Oh, yeah!" I said, in a voice that sounded forcibly cheerful. "I cut my hair myself all the time. It was just getting too long."

"Right," she said. "Um, goodnight?"

I went to bed and finally fell asleep.

Chapter 3

AT THE ARCHIVES, I WAS ALLOWED TO CHOOSE WHICH TWO days of the week would be my "weekend." Hannah explained to me that it was best to take weekdays, because then all of the businesses in Quesnel would be open to run errands. At first I picked Tuesday and Wednesday. However, these were the same as Hannah's, and she looked genuinely distressed at the idea of sharing two days off with me, so I changed it to Monday and Tuesday.

The townspeople of Wells often made the hour's drive to Quesnel on their days off, because it housed the nearest real grocery store, hairdresser, doctor's office, and bank. But there were certain members of the community who avoided all contact with the bigger city, population 23,000.

Some people travelled there only once a month, or once a season, making careful rations of their groceries, supplementing with expensive produce and essentials from the general stores, and some hunted moose and caribou. And some people almost never went to town unless absolutely necessary, asking their friends and neighbours to fetch meagre supplies from town on their trips. The general aversion to society might have seemed like an affectation if everyone wasn't so committed to the bit even when no one was around to see it.

On that first Sunday, my brand new "Friday," there was another concert, this time at the pub. I didn't go with Brandon to this one. He was there though, sitting at a long table beside the pool table, and he left his friends to say hello to me.

"You should introduce me to your friends," I said. I was feeling restless and a little stir-crazy, having meaningfully spent meaningful time with only Brandon and Hannah for almost a week.

Brandon nodded and said he would, but it was one of those things where you feel like someone rushes out of a conversation topic without you noticing, and somehow the matter is closed and you haven't gotten what you wanted. He returned to his friends.

I was watching the concert from the bar with Janine, who was one of Hannah's friends. I was supposed to go with Hannah, but she had decided to stay in. She was having an at-home date with Armand, a man with the grouchiest face I'd ever seen. By the looks of him, he was at least fifteen years her senior. He'd been in the kitchen when I'd arrived home from work that day.

"Oh!" I'd shouted when I came in. He'd glowered at me.

Hannah told me I should sit with Janine, who was expecting her and whom she had forgotten to cancel on.

At the pub, I met Janine, who wore a pastel-blue hat and grey T-shirt. She wrapped me in an enormous hug.

"Oh, are you not a hugger?" she asked.

I said I wasn't sure.

"Well, not everyone appreciates physical contact. Me? I love it, and I know how important it is. It literally produces hormones that make you happy. It's not for everyone though." She asked me where Hannah was.

"I think she's on a date," I said.

Janine seemed perplexed at this. "A date?"

"Yeah, with Armand?"

"Armand?"

"Oh, you don't know him either?"

"I had no idea, I don't know him."

I said I was sorry, I had assumed that she knew who he was, and that I hadn't meant to gossip or share information Hannah hadn't already shared.

Janine's face changed into a scowl. "Well, never gossip to me about Hannah, because she's one of the best people that I know."

"Oh, yeah." I felt a jolt, and covered for myself.

Janine reminded me of a certain type of person that I'd encountered for the first time when I went to McGill. They were mostly white, straight men and were usually residence advisors who began initiatives where they toured different buildings on campus and gave presentations about rape culture. Many of them had interesting haircuts that implied rich inner lives. With these people, you would enter into a normal conversation and leave with the feeling that you were socially inappropriate, or plagued by incurable internalized misogyny, or even very racist, and you wouldn't even know how it had happened, because you certainly hadn't said anything you felt was terrible at all. The next time you saw that person, you would be skulking before them, praying not to be implicated in anything unsavoury.

As Janine and I talked it became clear that she was interested in Hannah romantically.

"Hmmm, that must be why she hasn't been responding to my flirtatious messages," she said, showing me a wall of winky faces on her phone screen directed at Hannah's Facebook inbox. I felt a little bit sorry for Janine, because Hannah had already explained to me that she was not a lesbian, and the rainbow tattoo on her ankle was just a coincidence, thank you very much. Janine was in fact possibly one of the only gay people in town, which must have been difficult for her. For a second, I was overcome with tenderness toward her.

Janine put her phone away and drew my attention to Henrick, who was behind the bar, his hair looking especially dashing. I worried she was going to accuse me of having a crush on him.

"Too bad about what's going on with him, huh?" Janine said instead.

Relieved, I replied that I didn't know what was going on with him.

"Oh, it's just awful," she said, beckoning Henrick over to us. "How are things with Oksana?"

Henrick shrugged.

I thought for someone who was so judgmental about gossiping, Janine was very interested in whatever intrigue Henrick was involved in. Janine pointed Oksana out to me, with less discretion than I would have liked. I turned to see, and noticed a tall, gorgeous woman in lively conversation with some people I recognized as ArtsWells employees. She was, according to Janine, something of a prom queen in Wells: the successful director of ArtsWells, beautiful, outgoing, and well-liked by nearly everyone.

I turned back to Henrick, who for the first time appeared smaller and a little bit more vulnerable to me as he glowered at her from across the room.

When Henrick went into the back room, Janine explained to me that he had been secretly involved with Oksana for many months, and she had sworn him to secrecy about their liaisons.

"Apparently, she ended it with him last week and started dating some new guy from Cranbrook the very next day! Except, with this guy, she was happy to tell everyone about it!"

"Oh." I didn't think this sounded especially bad.

"She had no right to ask me to keep it a secret," said Henrick, who had re-entered the bar and was now crumbling coasters in his fingers. To retaliate against Oksana for dumping him, Henrick had told everyone in town about their secret affair. So Henrick was mad about being dumped, and Oksana was mad that he had told everyone they'd slept together.

"I just think it's a little bit messed up that she came here tonight," said Janine. "What do you think?"

"Uhhhhh." I tried to respond but instead took a big sip of my beer, which tasted like bread. "Seems like it."

Janine nodded her head as if proud of me. I had a bad habit of making statements in support of whoever I happened to be with at the time, probably to avoid disappointing them, or awkward conversations. Thus far, it had worked quite well in my favour, but I wondered if one day it would come back to bite me, and I would have to offer clarifications on my vague "Mmmhmmm"s and "Totally, I bet that's true"s.

The concert was overwhelming in general. The hotel pub was crowded; the band, the Interstellar Jays, were a beloved local trio made up of long-time residents of Wells, and it was as though everyone, literally everyone, in town came to see them, save the miners and shut-ins. They played klezmer-funk and wore kooky clothes: plaid vests, pageboy caps, maxiskirts. As they played, couples swing danced with wry, practised smiles on their faces. As they dipped and twirled, I was reminded of the banner photo of the woman in the Wells Facebook group.

Studying the room, I saw a woman's head turn — someone I thought I recognized. She looked like Barb Sharpe, my new therapist in Quesnel. I hadn't met her yet; my first appointment was to be in two days, on my "Sunday." I had selected her out of all of the therapists in town because she was the only woman, and the only one under fifty. I also liked her picture. I thought she was beautiful in a preserved and polished way, like the beauty of celebrities and television presenters.

Her website read, "You are capable of so much. Through gentle and compassionate collaboration with my clients, I create an environment where healing and achievement can happen."

Nothing wrong with that, I'd thought, selecting "book an appointment."

"I think that's my therapist," I said to Janine, straining to be heard over the klezmer beat.

"Pfffft, that's not your therapist!" said Janine confidently. She had become slightly boisterous now that the music was in full swing. She enclosed me in a bear hug.

• • •

On Tuesday, I made the drive to Quesnel to meet Barbara. This time I'd be driving there without my dad in the car ahead of me, and I had nightmare after nightmare the night before of making a wrong turn off a cliff.

Barbara's practice was situated in a room inside of a chiropractor's office. From the outside, it seemed like it was out of business, and I had to cup my hands and peer through the dark glass to confirm that it was open. The receptionist was a chipper woman who referred to me as "youse" and invited me to sit down in one of the mismatched chairs against the wall.

As Barb appeared and introduced herself to me with an extended hand, I was struck by her. She resembled her photo, but she also had an incredible warmth that I sensed immediately, and her voice was soft and feminine, like an early child educator or one of my mom's friends who my siblings and I would call "aunt." I wondered if this quality was innate within her, or it was something she had learned at therapy school.

Barb led me into her office at the back of the building; it was full of jewel-toned pillows and salt lamps. I sat on the couch, she on an armchair opposite, and our eyes met across the room.

"So," she began, "why did you decide to come to therapy today?"

"Well," I said, and I found myself thinking of an answer for a long time. I wanted to go to therapy because I believed it was one of those things that you should do if you had the money to do it. What's more, I did not know what was precisely wrong, but surely a seasoned professional could flush it out of me, whatever it happened to be.

"Well, I want to be more confident, I guess," I replied finally.

"Mmmm, always a great goal," she said, nodding vigorously. "Confidence. Wow. It's one of those huge things that can be so hard to find within ourselves." She clasped her hands as if she was trying to catch an imaginary wisp of confidence in front of her.

"Definitely," I said.

"Why don't you start by telling me a little bit about yourself?"

I explained to her that I was from Fenwick, Ontario, and that it was a very small town.

"Did you like growing up in a small town?" she asked.

"Not particularly," I said. "It was beautiful there, but I didn't really fit in with anyone and had a lot of trouble keeping friends, and it's fairly conservative." I told her about our member of provincial parliament, who was twenty-one and didn't believe in evolution.

"Wow," said Barb, "so not the smartest person ever."

"Yeah," I said, "not that I really noticed anything about politics until I had moved away for university. I wasn't super perceptive about that stuff as a child."

"Do you think children are supposed to notice and be perceptive about politics?"

"Smart ones are, probably."

"Hmmmm," said Barb. I told her more: how I had moved away to study at McGill in Montreal when I was eighteen, how I had done my master's in England, and how I came to be living in Wells.

"So now you're back in another small town," she said. "Wells is a *very* fascinating place. It's so incredibly diverse."

"Diverse?" I said. I thought Wells could be described in many ways, but diverse was not one of them. I could count on one hand the residents I had met thus far who were not white.

"Well, not in a traditional sense, of course, it is almost completely white, yes. But economically and from an education standpoint. There are accomplished, financially successful artists and wealthier nuclear families, and also individuals with less than a high-school education living below the poverty line."

"Really," I said, trying to apply this information to what I already knew and had seen of Wells. Since arriving, people had been pulling me aside or catching me alone and making bold statements about the nature of Wells, as if it were an organism with free will, or a megacity like New York or Paris: Wells was a small community full of life and incredible, unforgettable people. Wells was a vicious place dominated by small-town egos and politics. Wells was an escape from the hustle and bustle of everyday life, where you could get back to what it was all about. Wells was wrought with invisible poverty, mental illness, and alcoholism. You could live comfortably in Wells as an independent prospector of gold. Wells was on the brink of changing forever, and we'd never get it back or understand the enormity of our loss as a community.

So far, I'd heard more about what Wells was really all about, without actually experiencing that much. What wasn't I noticing?

"What do you think of it so far?"

"I don't know really," I said. "I think I might be having trouble fitting in."

"Have you made any friends yet?"

"Sort of. There's this guy Brandon, but I can't tell if he's trying to sleep with me."

"He wants to sleep with you?"

"That's what my roommate says, but I feel like she sometimes just says things to stress me out."

"Really?" Barb said, furrowing her brows, evidently taken aback.

"Well, maybe that's a mean-spirited thing to say about someone."

"Not if it's true," said Barb. "So, do you want to sleep with Brandon?"

"I don't know."

"You don't know?" She laughed a little, in a way that still sounded sweet. "What are you unsure about?"

"Um," I said, "everything?"

Barb leaned her head back and laughed a real laugh. "I'm sorry," Barb said. "Just the way you said it was funny."

"Oh, that's okay," I said wryly, trying not to beam after hearing that.

We discussed Brandon more. I told her he was an artist, and that he was pretty nice to me, and that he wasn't ugly. But it seemed to me that we were asking all the wrong questions. Wasn't it more important to figure out whether or not he liked me? Otherwise, what were we even talking about?

When my fifty-five minutes were up, Barb and I made a plan to meet every week. I initially suggested every two weeks, but Barb wanted to have more frequent sessions. "We can reduce once I've gotten to know you a bit better and you've had a chance to unpack everything."

I wondered if this was therapist code for "you are more mentally ill than you think," but was too afraid to ask.

I found myself thinking about Barb on the drive home, re-playing our session in my head with a mix of embarrassment and pleasure, and I realized that I forgot to ask her if she had been at the show.

As I drove, I felt a sense of calm fall over me, a quietness that I hadn't felt in a long time. In fact, I realized there were a few minutes where I wasn't thinking of much of anything at all, just marvelling at the foliage around me. I wasn't sure whether I could attribute this to my session with Barb, to my new-found alone time driving to and from Quesnel, or to the beautiful scenery and quiet surrounding me almost all the time since my arrival in the Cariboo. Maybe it was all three. Either way, it was nice to have something like a friend, even if she cost eighty dollars every week.

Chapter 4

ON WEDNESDAY, I WOKE UP TO FIND MY CAR COVERED IN A thick layer of ice. With no scraper, I ended up drawing a metal shovel over the windshield to remove the ice so I wouldn't be late for work. As the ice melted and dribbled down the windshield, I saw I had carved stark white lines horizontally along the window, like when you fold flimsy plastic too much. When I got home, Hannah asked me why I hadn't just used a credit card. I had no answer for her.

It was the last week of the tourist season. The park itself was nearly empty. Except for Germans, Nancy told me.

"Germans?"

"Germans make up a significant portion of our international visitors. They're very intrigued by mountains," she explained.

"I see. Don't they have the Alps?" I asked.

"I guess the Alps just make them want to see more mountains." During this final week that the park was open to the public I was allowed, and encouraged, to spend as much time in the park, or "in town," as I liked. Nancy told me this would give me a "crash course" on Barkerville. And indeed, the Germans who wandered around the park in pairs and family groups seemed especially excited to be there, talking in animated voices amongst themselves. As I wandered by one group, Lyle Smith, dressed as a lowly prospector, appeared and began his spiel on mining technology during the British Columbia Gold Rush.

"In town" the interpreters proved themselves to be a formidable bunch, meeting me with their most enthusiastic embodiments of living history, despite the season quickly coming to a close and the drastic weather changes. Jeremy, the handsome Wells firefighter, had rubbed soot from the wood-burning stoves around town to make himself resemble a real miner, straight from the shafts, donning a Scottish accent and, in character, referring to me only as "dear."

"I ken this place can be strange, but being out in nature seeking your fortune helps you appreciate a good scran at the end of the day," he said to me as he bit into a meat pie from the on-site bakery. At the end of each day, Jeremy and some other interpreters would gather in the street and sing recognizable folk songs: "Oh! Susanna," "The Belle of Belfast City," "Blackwater Side." Jeremy sometimes remained after they wrapped up and sang a little longer, making good-looking and meaningful faces at passersby as he sang "The Death of Queen Jane," a song he told me later he'd heard in the movie *Inside Llewyn Davis*.

Every day that week, I sat through two or three performances, tours, or demonstrations from the interpretation staff. I felt my head fill up with knowledge: how printing presses work, what women wore underneath their clothes in the Victorian and Edwardian periods, how Barkerville burned down entirely in 1868 and needed to be completely rebuilt. A kindly girl in the Chinatown school-house taught me how to write a translation of my name in Chinese calligraphy, explaining the strokes patiently and slowly to me. Back in the office, Nancy told me that the Chinatown in Barkerville never actually had a schoolhouse. The miners who immigrated from Guangdong almost never brought their families and did their best to return home as soon as possible. The school was created so that children would have an activity to do in Chinatown.

On the town tour, I learned that "Hurdy Gurdy girls" were dancers who travelled from town to town in indentured servitude to an enterprising man, charging five cents for a dance with one of his beautiful ladies, and that it was important that they be referred to and thought of as dancers only, not sex workers.

After these performances I would return to the administrative building feeling saturated with information, but by the next morning it was always hard to recall the many factoids and bits of wisdom I had received, as if they had trickled out of my ears onto the pillow while I was sleeping.

I was most nervous to see Brandon's friends, who portrayed the judges in the "Richfield Courthouse." We were all around the same age, and I wanted them to like me.

I went to see them on the final day the park was open. Richfield was actually a different town altogether during the gold rush, but now the courthouse was all that remained. It was three kilometres from Barkerville, up a steep path winding its way into the mountains. During the busy season, a stagecoach ran between the court-house and Barkerville, but it was no longer available. Every day, the boys donned their long black robes and traversed the town, disappearing into the woods on their way to the courthouse.

If you went to Richfield on foot, you were supposed to go with a friend, and talk to them the entire time to avoid surprising bears, said Ivan the blacksmith. He explained that the worry about bears wasn't that they would hear you and try to find and eat you, but that you would turn a corner and surprise one, which would upset it and make it want to kill you.

Since I didn't have a friend, Ivan advised me to fasten a bell to my waist or to sing a song.

With no bell either, I set off on the journey singing "Dream a Little Dream of Me" over and over again, hoping I wouldn't be overheard by either bears or people.

The path winded along a steep cliff, surrounded by coniferous trees and revealing the textured rock along the cliffside. I did not meet with any bears, but I did see an abandoned mine shaft, framed with wood. The air was somehow even more delicious smelling, and I was struck by a potent envy for the judges, who got to be friends and see one another every day, and travel this beautiful path together.

At the end of the path sat the courthouse, a wooden structure with a white clapboard exterior. Beside it was a bench with a plaque commemorating an actor who had spent twenty years performing the role of Judge Matthew Baillie Begbie and who had died recently. I wondered if this plaque intimidated the new guy playing Judge Begbie. What if he spent twenty years as Judge Begbie, and then died, and didn't get his own plaque?

I was the only spectator for the judges' performance. They didn't have quite the same approach to historical interpretation as the interpreters down the hill in Barkerville. The judges, who I understood were theatre students from the "lower mainland," seemed to be more influenced by the expressionistic sensibilities of *Looney Tunes* than by a desire to impart a faithful impression of the historical realities of early Canadian justice. They put on a slapstick version of a murder trial, in which Judge Begbie sentences a man to death. Greg Chapman portrayed the defendant and all the witnesses, replacing wigs and hats on his head frantically to accommodate the madcap switches within the story.

After the show, the judges hurried into the backroom together, and I heard lively chatter and uproarious laughter. I lingered for a few minutes, inspecting the maps and artifacts on display in each room, hoping they might come out and we could have a conversation.

When they didn't appear, I left the courthouse and followed the path back to Barkerville, singing "A Whole New World" to myself. At the bottom of the path back in town, Lyle Smith, in character, was perched on a prop barrel, playing harmonica. We waved to each other, and he winked at me.

• • •

As days began to pass in Wells, I noticed that time elapsed in a way that was starkly different from any place I had ever lived before. It was as if, with each passing day, I was burrowing deeper into something safe, and isolated, and stagnant, like a bear into a cave in the fall time before winter. I wasn't sure if this feeling was due to the cold weather, which came on so drastically and plunged us into winter long before the end of October, or the repetitive nature of the days working in the archives, then going home for the night with maybe a stop at the pub for a drink or two, and then to bed at 10:00 p.m.

Before going to sleep at night, I often fantasized about being a local and the sense of belonging that might afford me. How long would I have to live here before people loved me, the way they loved Brandon, and Hannah, and Janine? One year? Two? They were greeted warmly everywhere they went, and people spoke about them as if their personalities and interests were very important, regardless of what they were.

Soon, October was almost gone, and it was time for the cabaret at the Sunset Theatre. I was to understand that this was a big deal. Brandon often spoke of it in vague terms.

"Oh, it's *wonderful*," Veronica said one day at the pub. "It's like a big talent show where everyone is welcome to show off their special creative talents every few months. Everyone goes!" Around her, other patrons nodded and made humming noises in agreement, as if they were all collectively remembering their favourite moments from cabarets past.

The night of the cabaret, Hannah wanted to head over to the Sunset Theatre early, because it often sold out and all the best seats would be taken quickly.

Armand, Hannah's date from my first week in town, was coming to the show, too. He had started spending a lot of time in Wells, watching movies or going to the pub with Hannah for dinner. I came into the kitchen that day and I found him, as I often did, sitting at the table, silent as the grave and scowling. He'd driven from Quesnel to come with us. Hannah came in from the living room, humming a tune to herself, and was surprised to see me. She was often surprised to see me, as if shocked that I hadn't packed it in and left town in the middle of the day.

Armand and Hannah rarely spoke in front of me. Sometimes, she acted embarrassed of Armand. He was not handsome, and, as she had pointed out to me many times, was almost old enough to be her father. But Armand did regard her with something like tenderness, and sometimes I saw her gazing back at him with the same expression.

The Sunset Theatre was built in the 1930s, and used to be a movie theatre. It didn't have a screen anymore, but it had a stage, and a mezzanine level that only people who were friends with the owner could climb into. On the walls were enormous printouts of mid-century movie posters. Jack Lemmon's face was terrifying up close; he had so many folds in his forehead.

When we were in our seats, Hannah got up and told me she was going backstage.

"Oh, why?" I asked.

"Well, I have to get ready to perform," she said, waving an explanatory hand.

"Oh, you're performing?"

"Um, yes?" We locked eyes. She looked expectantly at me, a triumphant glint visible in her eye.

"Oh, great, good luck."

After she left, I sat alone with Armand. I thought that surely he would feel uncomfortable in the silence and attempt to fill it, but he said nothing. I was relieved when Sharon and Ricky appeared and sat themselves beside us.

A disembodied voice presented itself.

"Laaayyyydies and Geee-ennntttleeemen," said the voice. Everyone laughed, because they knew whose voice it was. I laughed, too, even though the voice was unfamiliar to me. The voice introduced the cabaret and made a bunch of jokes, some of which I didn't understand because they referred to people I hadn't met yet. The audience was well lubricated and offered ample reaction to this overseer.

The first act was an older woman I recognized from the chili bake off, with stringy hair and a high turtleneck, who played violin. Her violin playing was neither good nor bad, and the crowd clapped politely, a stark contrast to the applause for the beloved emcee.

The next act was a comedy sketch by Jeremy, the judges, and a gaggle of other street interpreters. Their skit was about a couple meeting on a first date, and the girl turning out to be obsessed with going to raves. The woman playing the date pulled a bunch of glow sticks out of her jacket pockets and threw them everywhere.

The audience reacted strongly to this sketch. Some people engaged with the players onstage by shouting out comments, or laughed and slapped their knees, as if their relationship to the sketch was just as important as the sketch itself and it was even more important that we all know this.

Next, a teenage boy performed an original song on the guitar. He sang:

> *If we could just give peace a chance*
> *If we could all get up and dance*

Halfway through, he lost his place. We, the audience, sat and watched as he went back a few bars and started again. The cabaret was beginning to remind me of talent shows I'd experienced in elementary school. We began to offer small, half-hearted encouragement to the boy in cheers and shouts, although it seemed as though collectively we might have preferred it if he had simply quit.

There were maybe twenty acts over two hours, eight of which were skits by Jeremy's group. The crowd always laughed uproariously during the sketches, which began to make it difficult to tell whether or not they were actually very good. Regardless, by the last sketch I was laughing enthusiastically and crinkling up my eyes, craning my neck to see everyone else in the audience, hoping to catch someone's eye so that we could laugh together.

During each act, as with any live performance, I was painfully present, but after the show was done I could hardly recall any of them. They were like dreams, slipping away from me in a single waking second after feeling so memorable. I held a strong memory of Hannah, who'd played "Für Elise" very slowly, and bowed deeply at the end of her performance with a genuine smile. I also remembered Oksana, Henrick's ex-lover. She was exceptionally beautiful and tall, and she'd performed a Ukrainian folk dance in traditional dress. She received a standing ovation for being good at dancing but also, I suspected, for being beautiful and a real winner in general.

However, by design, the most memorable act was Jeremy's "Gold Pan Poetry." This was an explosive and recurring performance at the cabaret that I had heard about from many locals beforehand, in which Jeremy came onstage naked, holding only a tin gold pan in front of his genitals, shielding them from the audience's view. He then recited a filthy poem he'd written himself, about having sex with one woman or another. This particular poem compared a woman's body to the softly curving mountains of Bowron Lake Provincial Park, and considered her vulva to be as fertile and gold-bearing as Williams Creek in the nineteenth century. It produced uproarious applause and wolf whistles as he walked off the stage, baring his ass to us.

After the show, we all gathered in the lobby of the Sunset, where refreshments were sold and the performers shuffled out from backstage. The comedy troupe stood in the corner, looking cool like football players or the Rolling Stones, or the Rolling Stones if they had patchy goatees. We didn't stay long, because Armand's scowl made me, and apparently Hannah, concerned that he would start a fist fight.

"That was pretty cool, huh?" asked Hannah on the way home.

"Pretty cool."

"I'm tired," said Armand. Startled, I realized that this was the first time I had heard him speak, and I was taken aback by his strong Australian accent. Hannah patted him on the arm.

• • •

The cabaret marked a shift in Wells. Many of the seasonal workers, including lots of the interpreters, remained in town only to perform at the cabaret, and left town immediately after. All at once, even the next day, the pub was emptier, the evenings quieter, with fewer musical events and activities scheduled at night and on weekends. The interpreters and seasonal workers who did remain shifted into different roles. Jeremy went to work in the mines, no doubt gathering lived experiences to apply to his interpretation, and Brandon took a job in the administrative building doing social media marketing for Barkerville. He was offered a full-time position, but he left early every day. Everyone gave him a hard time about this. I asked him one day why he did it.

"Listen, if I'm not being productive what's the point in my being here? It's better for me *and* for Barkerville if I'm not collecting money for hours where I'm not actually doing anything." He said this hurriedly, as if his point was obvious, grabbing his things and preparing to go home to play *Red Dead Redemption 2* with his roommate, Hunter. Behind his back, I saw Hannah roll her eyes.

I considered arguing that he would make more money and help Barkerville more if he simply stayed and actually did his work, instead of just doing whatever he wanted. But I could not imagine that I had any power to change his mind, and I thought it might make him annoyed with me and not want to be around me anymore. Besides, he wouldn't be leaving early unless he really thought it was a normal and good thing to do, so it probably was anyway.

By this time, it was bitterly cold.

"We get a dry cold here," said Hannah, "so you can go outside and it knocks the wind out of you, but it doesn't get in your bones like a wet cold." I knew wet cold very well from the U.K., where in winter the humidity always made my bed and my clothes, meant to be cozy, feel damp 24/7, as if someone had peed on them a few hours before.

I started waking up with a sore throat each morning due to the dryness, and would cough an enormous wad of phlegm into the sink. I went to a doctor, and he told me there was nothing he could do. Besides, the only real problem with my post-nasal drip was that it was gross. I drank what felt like hundreds of cups of hot water with lemon, ginger, and honey a day.

Around the same time, I received an email notifying me that I had received my final master's thesis grade. I had been awarded a 66, which in the United Kingdom denoted a grade of "merit." This meant my thesis was good, but one step down from "distinction." I was both pleasantly surprised and disappointed by this grade.

The critical feedback from each of the adjudication board members was one or two lines, indicating that my writing, content, structure, formatting, and use of primary texts were good, but not great, without any additional information about what made it good but not great. It was as if the adjudicators had recognized my lack of effort and enthusiasm for my thesis and had chosen to put just as much effort into their feedback. I called my mom and told her this.

"You know what, sweetheart?" my mom said. "They probably just gave you merit because they're jealous of your academic skill. It happens all the time." I considered this and determined that it was almost certainly untrue, but said that maybe she was right. I hung up, having gained no new perspective or information.

I told Hannah about my grade, and she told me that she had received the highest mark in her undergraduate class and had been able to recite entire Old English romances at that time.

"Not anymore though."

"That's too bad," I said.

The day after I received my marks, Hannah and I learned that we would have a new roommate. Her name was Logan and she was moving into the staff house at the end of the month. She was hired as a graphic designer, an exciting and new position for Barkerville, for which they had been awarded a grant.

I was impressed by the fact that this person was a graphic designer, as it was a skill I had seen on many job postings, and it had always seemed just out of my grasp. It always seemed like I would need to spend three years, or ten thousand dollars, to become anything close to a graphic designer.

Nonetheless, when I learned Logan was coming, I got a horrible knot in my stomach. I was afraid that Logan, who I thought was very beautiful in her LinkedIn photo, would take something from me when she arrived. I had only just begun to get a handle on my new situation, and in a life as small as the one I led in Wells, a new roommate was titanic. I had just learned that I would likely never be an above-average academic. I wasn't sure I could handle being the second-newest girl in town.

Despite that, I was also relieved to get a new roommate, because I was beginning to suspect that Hannah didn't like my company much at all.

Whenever I told Hannah I was going to the store, or on a walk, or to pick up toilet paper when I went out, she simply and consistently responded "okay?" It was as if her ultimate goal was to teach me that most of the time what I had to say was actually unnecessary, and I was beginning to internalize this message, choosing my words and expressions carefully, only speaking to her when I was absolutely sure she needed to hear it.

And as much as I could play the victim in my own mind about our dynamic, I didn't quite understand Hannah myself. Sometimes she called me over to her desk to show me videos she found funny. They were usually of people singing opera badly, which I didn't find funny at all, because opera was really hard and you needed to have a lot of training to do it well. It felt like laughing at a child trying to drive a car.

"Did you study opera?" I asked, wondering if I was missing an important piece of this puzzle.

"Gosh, no, my voice isn't nearly nice enough," she said wistfully. "I *wish*."

Once, Hannah said she had something even cooler than bad opera singers to show me.

"You'll *love* this," she said. She turned on the video. What followed was a recording of Hannah herself, with a different haircut, playing a song on the piano.

She stared at me, waiting for my response. I watched. The song was certainly quite pretty and she played it very well, but I'd heard her play nicer songs on the piano at the staff house before.

I furrowed my brow and squinted to see closer, while also trying to appear impressed.

"That's a great song," I said, when the video was done, "and you play it really well."

"Isn't that so *cool*?" she asked with emphasis.

We stared at one another.

For the first time, I was sufficiently moved to say "um, okay?" Hannah was slowly breaking me down, taking me to her level.

I called my brother, David, and told him about this predicament with Hannah.

"You need to stop letting tall women torture you," he reasoned. He always gave succinct advice.

I did appreciate and truly admire Hannah's relationship to her work, and to the past in general. She appeared to genuinely understand how to engage with history, how to massage information out of artifacts that I would have taken at face value as useless or unimportant. This was true of many of my co-workers, except for maybe Brandon.

Evidently, I was not a gifted scholar, and I wondered if perhaps I would not be an exemplary museum and heritage employee after all, not destined, as I had secretly dreamed, to become an ingenue curator, running my own museum before my thirties. I did the tasks that Nancy and Hannah assigned me, but about a month into my time, I did not have any truly exciting ideas or feelings about Barkerville, and I found myself struggling to absorb information and learn new things about it that hadn't already neatly packaged for my consumption by the interpreters.

My problem, I suspected, was my obsession with stories. When I thought about Barkerville I mostly considered how its history might be neatly transformed into a novel or mini-series. It was easy enough to imagine an incredible romantic story about a Hurdy Gurdy girl gaining her independence from her cruel employer by marrying a handsome miner, as in the tale of Bella Hodgkinson, a nineteenth-century resident of Barkerville and the historic persona of the interpreter who did the town tour. But finding this story in marriage and death records and deed transfers in the first place was something else entirely.

For that, I had to respect Hannah, who I could pretend to be superior to because I found her personality confusing, but who ultimately could hold her own in the world in a way I could not, and at twenty-six, too. She would be fine; she knew where she belonged.

• • •

Logan arrived the day before Barkerville was to open for its annual Halloween weekend. This was fitting, because she looked like a vampire, at least much more so than her LinkedIn picture suggested she would. She was tall and pale and had a long white face with grey and purple eyeshadow. Her hair was dyed dark red, almost purple, and fell almost to her bum, and she even wore a V-neck shirt with a skull on it. She reminded me of Anne Boleyn, or some beautiful medieval noblewoman. When she said hello her voice was surprisingly high and youthful, with a Canadian twang that made her seem younger than her age of thirty.

She had driven to Wells from Vancouver with her boyfriend, Matt. Matt was much shorter than her, and he had a handsome face and a body that suggested that he worked out a lot. I thought they looked a little strange together. I thought about how someone like my older sister, or maybe Janine, or any competent, worldly person might feel very confident in that assessment, and repeat it to someone else in a hushed tone. But when Matt reached for Logan's hand as they wandered through the house I was reminded that I knew little about love.

Matt stayed the night. I felt guilty for having taken the double room, because Logan had to claim the single bed.

"Oh, don't worry about it!" Logan said cheerily when I apologized. She genuinely didn't seem to care about this, and nothing she did or said indicated that she thought she'd been cheated into an unfair deal.

In the morning, Hannah, Matt, Logan, and I all went out for breakfast at the Wells Hotel. There we saw Brandon and his roommate Hunter. They joined us and told us all about *Red Dead Redemption 2*, which Logan had heard of and was looking forward to playing herself. They launched into conversation. The knot tightened again. Why hadn't I thought to develop an interest in video games? All of a sudden, I was gripped with a vision of my life in Wells, playing second fiddle to Logan. I imagined the rest of my time there, with Brandon's interest transferred to Logan, and me behind her, the second to speak and second to be spoken to.

"You can feel so out of place when you're the oldest one at the table," Hannah said, addressing me but talking into her coffee mug.

"But Logan is thirty," I explained. Hannah looked at me meaningfully, her eyes twinkling. I had never seen her happier. She didn't speak for what felt like a long time. I wanted to wave my hands in front of her face and say "hellooo?"

"I can't believe you fell for it," said Hannah.

"Are you not twenty-six?" I asked, turning to everyone else at the table, who had not been listening.

"I'm thirty-four!"

"Okay."

"Wow, you really believe everything you hear." She turned to Hunter and Logan and Brandon, her mouth a conspiratorial grin. They politely returned her gaze, happy to laugh at a joke if someone was making one.

"Well, you lied." I wanted to shake her. Hannah, as ever, was a mystery to me. Everything she did made me feel like I was living on Neptune. And yet I was sorry for her, because somehow it seemed that she really wanted to be twenty-six.

She kept saying that she didn't like the guy she was dating that much, and that she wanted to travel, and have kids, and buy a house. I was ten years away from being thirty-four. Who was I going to be at that time? Would I be having breakfast with a bunch of people I didn't like and lying about my age?

In truth, what opportunity did Hannah have for change up here in the mountains? Since being here, nothing exciting had happened to me at all, except for shows at the pub and the Sunset Theatre, and seeing the same fifty people over and over again. It was difficult to fathom leading that type of life for four years like she had. She couldn't go to school, or start a real business, or work her way up the corporate ladder, or meet new people who would challenge and excite her. She couldn't even go to church, even though she'd told me that was important to her, because the last church had been shut down five years ago due to lack of attendance and financial troubles.

And yet there was a lulling pull from Wells, something whispering in my ear, telling me that it was safe here and that I could stay here forever. I somehow thought that I could take my pants off and take a shit in the middle of the restaurant if I wanted to. It would be embarrassing, but only about two hundred people would ever hear about it, and when I left the event would stay here, and I could leave it behind. Wasn't there some freedom in that? Was that what drew Hannah in?

The waitress came and took our orders. Hannah ordered her eggs poached hard.

• • •

Logan, I quickly learned, was vivacious and friendly. As I'd feared, people really liked her. Since it was the weekend before Halloween, the park was going to open for two days only for a haunted house and other seasonal activities like pumpkin carving and a "hayride," which was actually just a carriage ride down Main Street, with no real hay involved.

Logan and I were both recruited to help set up and run the events, and we were sent over to the visitors' centre to sift through boxes of decorations and fold pamphlets. From the other side of the visitors' centre, I could see her laughing with Rhoda, the exceptionally square-jawed receptionist who worked in the administrative building. I felt like such a fool. I had not even considered trying to befriend Rhoda, as I didn't think she would find me interesting, and because she always responded "oh, I'm just ducky" whenever I asked her how she was, but in a sarcastic tone which made me feel like she wasn't really ducky at all and like I shouldn't ask any more questions.

How could I have overlooked Rhoda, who now seemed to me very interesting and not intimidating at all? I didn't think we had ever laughed together, not even once. I tried to make myself feel better by reminding myself that Timothy, the elusive, elderly curatorial assistant who always made stew on a hot plate in the kitchen at lunch, once asked me into his office so he could show me a prank video of someone putting "fart spray" into a box to surprise a serial package thief.

When people asked Logan about herself, she didn't cast her eyes down at the ground or say "um, I guess," or shuffle her feet or appear sullen at all, despite her goth exterior. She was perky and breezy.

I was paired up with Veronica from the visitors' centre, and Sharon, Nancy's boss, assigned us to be in charge of the face-painting station. Sharon didn't seem to think it was a big deal that I had never painted a face in my life.

"You'll be great." She assured me when I protested. She handed us a box of paint and brushes and sparkles and left us alone. Children lined up behind us. One kid asked for Charlie Brown on his cheek, but what I painted just resembled a planet of some kind. A little boy dressed like Captain America wanted me to put a bullet hole on his forehead. I asked Veronica whether she thought we could do that.

"I think it sounds quite creative," she said to the little boy. I painted the bullet hole in the middle of his forehead, with a thick trickle of blood coming out. Doing this made me feel like a criminal, like I was actually shooting the little boy.

Veronica told me about herself, and I made sure to listen closely and not to overlook her. She was going to the Calgary comic con in the spring, where she was going to meet up with a guy from Red Deer she'd been internet dating since August.

"He wants to take things slow," she said, pulling up his Plenty of Fish profile and presenting a photo of a man in a truck smoking a cigar with a cowboy hat on.

Veronica also showed me a photo of herself wearing an impressive handmade costume. The outfit included breastplates resembling the domed head of the droids, like she had beheaded two R2D2s and turned them into a bra.

Later, when I was done my shift, I saw the boy with the bullet hole on Main Street. His cheeks rosy from the cold, he was being hotly pursued by his father who kept pretending to shoot him in the head. Each time, the boy fell to the ground in heaps of laughter, which rang out through the crisp fall air to the very edges of the park.

Brandon had been responsible for decorating the haunted house, which he said was "Nightmare Before Christmas" themed. In reality, Barkerville didn't have a budget for any new decorations that could align with his intended theme, so the real theme was "mannequins." At the end of the night, Brandon came up behind me and tried to push me toward the haunted house.

"Ready to get scaaaared?" he said.

I moved to the side quickly and said, "no no no!" This made Janine, Logan, and Ricky, who were working inside the haunted house, break character and laugh uncontrollably, although I wasn't sure why.

Throughout the next week, Ricky would keep saying "No no no!" in a high-pitched voice whenever I saw him around town. I would do my best to smile back, unsure of what he wanted me to say.

. . .

On Saturday night, Logan, Hannah, and I went to a Halloween party at the Hubs Motel, a somewhat seedy looking joint where out-of-towners stayed when the hotel was full or they were on a budget. I dressed as the Paper Bag Princess and Logan was a cat. Hannah didn't dress as anything. The entire town came out. They'd set up the motel as a trick-or-treating route for children, who could knock on the doors, each with a different theme, and receive candy. I supposed one of the benefits of being such a small community was the capacity to organize things like that. Indeed, all the children and parents knew each other.

The children in Barkerville, I came to learn, had curious and often animal-themed names: Griffin, Finch, Maijia, Lion. Their parents were the Gen-X creatives and free-spirits who built their families here. A group of women ushered Logan and me up the stairs and offered us Jell-O shots.

"It's so hard to explain to Maijia why she can't have these — she thinks they're treats!" said Melissa, who'd grown up in Wells and worked in the administrative building in the winter and as an interpreter in the summer. She was in her forties and was exceptionally attractive with her clear olive skin. "I told her it's Mommy's special snack that isn't good for kids." We all leaned our heads back and laughed.

I noticed that Logan made simple jokes, ones that were easy for everyone to understand and appreciate. When Sheena, another middle-aged interpreter who wore little half-moon glasses and flowy maxi-dresses in her day-to-day life, accidentally dropped her Jell-O shot cup off of the landing by accident, Logan was quick to point it out, and we all laughed together at Sheena's mistake.

Hannah was especially taken with Logan. When Cabaret and the Halloween events were over, she invited her to Quesnel with her.

"Josie, you like going by yourself. Logan and I can go together today," she said, a forced smile on her lips.

"I don't really," I said, "I just thought you wanted to go alone." Hannah pretended she hadn't heard me.

"Sure, I'd be happy to go with you!" said Logan to Hannah cheerfully, oblivious to the advanced emotional politics taking place between Hannah and me. I watched with envy as Hannah's van pulled out of the driveway, even though I hadn't really wanted to go to town with Hannah anyway, and I did like going alone.

Later in the week, Hannah, Logan, and I watched *Fatal Attraction* together. Initially, Hannah said she wouldn't watch it.

"It's misogynistic," she said curtly.

Hannah was a curious woman in that she held many conflicting opinions inside of her spindly frame, and somehow there was room for all of them. She would not watch Glenn Close depict an anti-feminist character in *Fatal Attraction*, and yet she did not believe women should get abortions unless they reaaaaaaally needed one or that there should be scholarships for people with marginalized identities.

"It doesn't make any sense," she said. "Like, most of the time you can't even tell when someone is gay, or half Black, or whatever. Why should we reward people for things that don't matter anyway?" I wanted to remind her that, as a historian, she could see in the evidence that these things did matter and made a big difference in how someone's life turned out. But Logan was nodding and furrowing her brow intensely as she listened to Hannah, as if she was saying something very intelligent. Hannah was one thing, but I didn't think I could argue with both of them at once. If someone believes something in their heart, how on Earth can you change their mind?

Hannah changed her mind about the movie when she realized that Logan really wanted to watch it. I opened my laptop and turned on the film. Things went quite well for a few minutes, until I remarked that Glenn Close, whose beauty was quite challenging in photographs, was actually effortlessly stunning when you saw her move onscreen.

"It's something about the way she moves and her voice, it's strange," I said.

Logan said it was an insightful thing to say. "Wow, you know I've *never* thought of that before. That is *so* true. She doesn't seem beautiful in pictures. But she is."

"What does it matter if she's attractive," said Hannah, "if she's a talented actress?" She glared at us for a minute before standing abruptly. "You know, I don't think I'm in the mood to watch this anymore," she said, and went quickly to her room.

Logan and I sat solemnly for some time together, gazing at the floor quietly, before turning our attention and conversation, quieter this time, back to Glenn and her unique beauty.

After that, Hannah stopped inviting Logan to do activities with her. Logan and I began to spend more time together, taking drives to Quesnel without Hannah, who was always "busy" with chores, and going to the pub in the evenings. Logan liked to get challenging IPAs.

I found Logan to be a surprising person; I could never assume her opinions. For instance, she did not believe it was appropriate or ethical to take down statues and monuments of problematic, controversial, or otherwise unsavoury historical figures.

"It's like erasing *history*," she said, throwing her arms in the air one evening on the couch. "People need to get a life!" She was referring to the statue of Judge Matthew Baillie Begbie that had been recently slated for removal from the law society in Victoria, her hometown.

I had accidentally ignited this debate when I mentioned seeing an article about it on CBC's website. Because Logan and I were both women of similar age, and I thought we both seemed pretty smart, I assumed she felt the exact same way about it.

I had spent so much time in my undergraduate degree and during my master's around people with exactly the same views as me that I found myself at a loss as to how to explain why I thought I was right, which made me unsure if I was actually right at all. Everything I said came out weakly, and unconfidently.

"Logan, I just don't think that's true," I said now, but I was somehow powerless to argue against her further, unable to think of any robust arguments to make that would sway her; she was so confident in herself.

The thing about university was that you could make people perform the right opinions about any topic by making them feel like an inherently bad person. The threat of a well-crafted Facebook post or otherwise public call-out about problematic behaviour ever-looming, we all naturally fell into line regarding the status quo.

I didn't know if this was a good thing or a bad thing, but I at least understood how to navigate political ideas within that framework. In the presence of Logan and her scattered political allegiances, I was baffled, having no way to compell her to agree with me.

Despite our differences, Logan and I grew closer and closer. I couldn't very well act chilly toward her, because she was always there, being kind to me and offering to give me one of her pudding cups or to accompany me on a walk.

I realized how close Logan and I were becoming at our first staff meeting. Because the curatorial department was so big, we held the meeting in a building that had been renovated inside to host school groups. It had a big wall of chalkboards and many desks, which we arranged in a big square.

Before the meeting began, Sharon stood in front of the chalkboards and instructed us to anonymously write something we admired about each person in the room on individual sticky notes, and to deposit them on each other's desks. I didn't know anyone particularly well at that point, and found myself writing elaborate and detailed praises about everyone in the room on the tiny pieces of paper. Following this, Sharon invited us all to read the comments out loud to the entire room. I watched, humiliated, as Charles, who was the development officer at Barkerville and who sported an obscenely long ponytail, read my note.

"You ... are ... an inspiration?" he read out loud, his eyes darting around the room searching for the person responsible. I averted my eyes and concentrated hard on my pile of sticky notes.

Most of mine were about not knowing me very well, but saying that nonetheless I seemed really nice and sweet. People often tell me I'm sweet, even though when they say this I'm sometimes thinking something evil, like hoping a love rival falls down the stairs or that someone's creative project or batch of brownies turns out poorly. I often thought evil things, but no one ever noticed or knew.

I came to one that read, "I don't know what I'd do without you, girl!" I turned my head to see Logan, who met my eye and did a dance with her eyebrows, smiling warmly at me. This made me incredibly happy, like being on a plane that was just landing.

My final sticky note read, "You have a mischievous twinkle in your eye ;)."

We sorted through several slated and unslated projects for the curatorial department, most of which were not financially attainable. The ultimate goal for Barkerville was to be designated a UNESCO World Heritage Site, which would funnel millions of extra dollars into the park for development. To do this, we would need to create a unique and innovative experience of lived history during the gold rush that had never been done at any museum.

Many members of the staff, especially Timothy and Hannah, emphasized that we had to fight the *Disneyfication* of Barkerville at all costs, although it was unclear where those efforts were coming from, or how we might combat them. Each member of staff was very passionate about the issues they spoke about, from replacing the roofing on the Kwong Sang Wing house to creating "Barkerville After Dark" programming.

By the end of the meeting, it was clear that the funds we had for the curatorial department this year would be going toward mundane and long-overdue repairs, with all of the more interesting or progressive projects shunted forward to another season in the unclear future.

I watched with admiration as Sharon facilitated this four-hour meeting. She was a stern person, with few smiles to share with the group and little interest in small talk and ice breakers. But she pushed us along, encouraging us to move from one topic to the next with confidence, and she made it look easy.

Chapter 5

AFTER LOGAN'S NOTE TO ME IN THE TEAM MEETING, I BE-
came aware that she and I were becoming a duo, like the ones in movies
about teenage girls. Soon, our routines were conjoined, and wherever
we went, we went together. I had not yet learned that in adulthood,
there are fewer and fewer opportunities to platonically link your life to
someone else's, unlike in school and even university where this could
happen five hundred times with a thousand different people. All of a
sudden you and some friend would be having sleepovers every night,
and you were the friend who got to go to the amusement park with
them. That was what was happening between Logan and me.

"So nice to see you girls spending so much time together,"
Veronica said to us when we went to the café in the visitors' centre
for lunch. We beamed back at her.

I found Logan to be a challenging and genuinely unique person. I learned new things about her every day, and revelled in our rare similarities when they made themselves evident. I was delighted to learn that before she became a graphic designer, she had trained to be a car mechanic, but quit due to issues she had with the industry. To have "issues" with an entire industry seemed incredibly grown-up and wise to me, and I wondered if one day, if I left the museum industry, I, too, could say it was due to "issues" I had with it. It sounded so smart.

Logan and I were both a bit taken aback to learn that Remembrance Day was a big deal in Wells. It was important to Hannah, and everyone in town, that we all attend the ceremony at the Legion. I wasn't quite sure why we even had a Legion, since I was pretty confident that there were no veterans in town, but they had good poutine.

At the ceremony, Charles, his ponytail twisted into a respectful bun, read a solemn poem and speech that he had penned himself about the Second World War, his voice warbling cinematically like Justin Trudeau's at his father's funeral. Hannah bowed her head, as if in deep thought. Logan and I caught one another's eye. Logan made a face, which I thought was bold for Remembrance Day, but I respected it because I, too, was confused at the intensity of emotion on display all around me. In university, I had learned to be skeptical of this type of patriotism and outward glorification of combat while our country was still involved and supplying weapons to many conflicts around the world.

In the evening, we were all encouraged to go see what we were told was a special performance of *Vincent's Promise*, a play written and performed by a local woman and directed by her husband. According to the pamphlet we were given, this play had been performed hundreds of times all over the country and even on Vimy Ridge and Juno Beach.

The play was about a jaded veteran who had lost his brother in battle, and a little boy in France charged with tending to the war memorial in his town, both portrayed with blinding earnestness by the playwright. The play, the entire day, reminded me of elementary school, performing solemnity about something that had not been fully explained to me, or was rather explained in an abstract way, without providing all of the details. It was a relief to know that Logan felt the same way, but I thought we might be the only ones. At the end of the performance, I snuck a glance around the room at the many wet eyes in the audience.

Logan was much better with people, and especially men, than I was. She had only been here a couple of weeks and had already developed particular friendships with Jeremy, Hunter, and Brandon, with the former inviting her over to his home to watch horror movies, a genre they both loved, on Wednesday nights. I was so jealous of her, but when I imagined myself in her place I couldn't imagine what Jeremy and I could possibly talk about.

"Do you think Jeremy has a crush on you?" I asked her at the bar after the play, where the audience as well as the playwright and director had convened.

"Pffffft, no," said Logan. "Besides, he's not my type at all."

She didn't seem invested in the idea of Jeremy having a crush on her, which was confusing to me. I desperately wanted to be more like Logan, and to seek out these respectful mutual connections with men. Maybe it was that I didn't have many male friends and found it difficult to make them, but I got the sense that men were more valuable friends to have than women, even though I liked most of the women I met better than the best men I knew. I felt guilty for thinking of things that way, but I could tell by the way other women my age responded when a man entered conversation that they probably felt that way, too.

The director of the play, the playwright-actor's husband, approached the bar and stood beside me. I turned to face him. He had wild, full hair and wore a sweater that reminded me of Kramer in

Seinfeld. I was three drinks deep and thought maybe he and I could talk, and maybe he'd become my male friend. *After all, I used to be a director, too*, I thought. Envisioning a charming mentor-mentee situation in which he uncovered my hidden genius for blocking and light design, I opened my mouth to speak.

"You directed *Vincent's Promise*, didn't you?"

The director turned to me with an expression I couldn't identify.

"Oh, you directed *Vincent's Promise*, didn't you?" he said, flopping his hands in front of himself, like Trump mocking the reporter. "Like, I *so totally* did, it was so *fabulous*." His tone took on the intonation of my own voice, with its inexplicably Californian bent that men so often pointed out to me. I did not know what to do, so I told him I had directed a few plays myself.

"How *so* totally cool. I bet you just *loved* directing plays."

"You know, I did," I said. The director snorted at me, was given his pint, and then returned to his table where he was sitting with his wife along with Sheena and Melissa. I turned to watch them. The playwright and I made eye contact. She was stunning, and looked happy and comfortable. She put her hand on the director's shoulder, and he said something that made her laugh a lot. Were they talking about me?

I turned my attention back to Logan, who looked confused.

"He was making fun of me, wasn't he?" I asked.

"Seems like it. What on Earth?" I was relieved that Logan had also seen this and confirmed my experience. I noticed that often when someone that everyone likes or who is talented acts like an asshole, people pretend they don't notice it or refuse to believe your account of it.

• • •

I discussed this incident with Barb the next time I saw her. She encouraged me to consider the experience in a more holistic way, not because he wasn't being an asshole, but because it might help me to suffer less when I thought about it.

"You say he directed a play, so maybe he's an actor, and he was just trying out a new persona for a character he's developing," she suggested. "Maybe you *inspired* him." Barb could never understand that this was not the type of thing that would happen to me, because she was so happy and sexy and probably inspired people all the time.

"Yeah, maybe." I paused. "What is it about me that invites that type of behaviour, do you think?"

"Maybe everyone experiences things like this, but you just don't know about it," she said, "and maybe you react more strongly to it than other people, or they react strongly but keep it a secret."

I considered this, but it meant nothing to me. In any case, I hated the director and would never forgive him for making fun of me, and I wanted his future creative endeavours to be poorly received.

"Why does he get to take up space creatively, but I don't?" I asked Barb.

"Sounds like he tries to take up space, and people let him. Do you try to take up space with your creativity?" I had to admit that I didn't. In the past, I'd written down things that had happened to me, or made up stories that I believed accurately captured how I felt about a given thing. I always loved them and would reread them over and over. Then, a friend and I agreed to swap our writing and offer feedback to each other. He'd told me my writing was so bad that he couldn't properly critique it, because I was such a sweet person and my existence brought so many people joy that hurting me was too hard for him. Since then, I hadn't been writing much, just nursing my embarrassment in private.

"I feel like men are always hiding some deep-seated anger at me, like they want to hurt me." I tried to find words to explain this better, but I couldn't. "They just ... find me disgusting."

"They find you *disgusting*?" asked Barb, seeming genuinely in-credulous. "Is it maybe possible that not every man hates you? Or finds you disgusting?" She paused. "And maybe some men, like Brandon, are actually attracted to you?" Barb was doing the thing she often did where she makes me admit that something is not one hundred percent a certain way, in order to enhance my mental flex-ibility in the face of adversity.

"Yeah, maybe," I conceded, although this didn't make me feel much better. There were always outliers.

"I wish I wasn't so sensitive," I said, emotional suddenly, my eyes welling up. I reached for a tissue on the end table and blew my nose, before laughing a big self-conscious laugh. "This is so stupid. He's just some random guy."

"Yeah, well," said Barb in a relaxed voice. "If you weren't sensi-tive then you wouldn't be you, and then where would you be?"

"Somewhere amazing, I bet."

• • •

Going to town was my favourite part of the week. Logan and I always went together on Tuesdays. Logan liked driving, too, but I always offered to drive both ways both because I enjoyed it, and because sometimes she drove really fast and didn't seem to mind where the lines on the road were. I started to imagine us in the far future, into my late twenties and her thirties, making this trip again and again. The repetition and strict scheduling reminded me of summer camp, or of being at an exclusive re-treat where routine was meant to heal your messed up gut or your divorce trauma. It became a secure, unshakable part of my life. No matter what happened in a given week, I knew I'd be going to Quesnel with Logan in a few days, and we would get lunch.

While I had therapy in town, Logan always read a book at Granville's Coffee. Logan was, by any definition, a voracious reader. She read at least two books a week, unless she was reading something very long, like *Anna Karenina* or *A Little Life*, her most recent book. She was proud of the fact that she had read *Mein Kampf*, as had Hannah for some reason, and the two of them had discussed the unique feeling of bringing your copy of *Mein Kampf* out to read in public and having people stare at you for it. They'd rolled their eyes in tandem, relishing this dilemma, emphatically agreeing that, of course, it wasn't for pleasure, it was for a love of history.

On one of our trips to town, Logan revealed to me that she had dyslexia, and so she was working tirelessly to catch up with everyone around her. I, on the other hand, read probably six books a year and was privately very proud of it. I wondered if I would waste my time wondering whether men found me disgusting if I had dyslexia to contend with.

Our weeks were organized around these trips. We discussed them in minute detail all week: Where would we go? What did we need to buy? Where would we have lunch? Then, on the way back, we'd discuss the next week's trip, and grocery items we'd forgotten to get, and gossip about people in town. I always forgot my reusable grocery bags, and Logan always remembered hers and lent me some.

A trip to town usually included a visit to the Quesnel library, and to Books and Company, the only bookstore in town. We had tried to get library cards at the Wells Public Library in early November. The regular librarian had been out recovering from hip surgery. The replacement librarian, a sixty-five-year-old woman in a Tweety Bird sweater, tried to issue us library cards but had trouble navigating the computer system.

"This thing, it's being such a frickin' nerd." She kept repeating this insult, smacking the faded white plastic monitor of the enormous, ancient computer. "A frickin' nerd," she said, until her face went red and I grew worried for her. We thanked her for her time and excused ourselves.

This was okay, because the Wells Public Library mostly stocked John Grisham and romance novels, and if you wanted something different you had to order it in and wait weeks to get it. After all, Wells and Barkerville were situated at the end of a long road, not on the way to anywhere but the wilderness, and it was probably pretty annoying even for an interlibrary courier to have to make the trip to deliver *The Memory Keeper's Daughter*.

Logan and I always wore nice outfits to town, and I sometimes wore mascara and eyeliner.

I relished every part of the journey, from gliding through the beautiful scenery and into town, sometimes seeing caribou or a porcupine, to the very end, when, if I needed it, I filled the tank up with gas at the station right before the great incline up into the mountains. The cold air was shocking as I stood still in the lot, looking around at the other drivers, comrades in transportation. Like me, I understood when our eyes met, their lives were made up of these small, chilly moments.

In the Cariboo, I was separated from nature by the thinnest of veneers. If I didn't get gas in Quesnel, my car could stop in the mountains, hours from Wells on foot. If it was late in the day, there might not be anyone nearby to pick us up, and we might freeze to death, or be eaten by wolves.

I loved the cold gas pump in my hand, how it made my fingers tremble, then go numb as I held the trigger down, watching the meter go up.

Logan always had intense reactions to the playlists I made for the drive, and I enjoyed trying to guess which songs she would like and which ones she would find ridiculous, or hilarious, or strange. She loved "I Took a Pill in Ibiza (Seeb Remix)" by Mike Posner, a song I was embarrassed to love and that she sang along with unself-consciously. Soon, I found myself joining in with her.

She balked at "Six O'Clock News" by Kathleen Edwards. "What kind of songs do you listen to, Josie?!" She smiled as if she had learned something terrible and hilarious about me.

I shrugged and tried to appear relaxed. I had no answer that would satisfy her. I thought "Six O'Clock News" was a pretty and sad song, and I liked listening to it a lot. Logan's reactions were so hard to predict and seemed arbitrary somehow, but nevertheless there she was, asking me to explain myself. I didn't dare play the "40s Country" playlist that I had loved so much during my thesis.

Logan teased me incessantly. She teased everyone. It was stressful and confusing, but it was such extreme attention paid to my person that I couldn't help feeling good about it later. I tried to be alert for times that she did teaseable things so that I could laugh at her, but I could see that everything she did and liked aligned with who she was as a person, and it didn't make sense to me to laugh at her for that.

Once, when we arrived in Quesnel, I parked and left the car without turning it off and left the keys in the ignition.

"Wait ..." Logan said. "Did you just ...?" I turned and saw what I had done.

"I did," I said.

"Did you forget to turn the car off?"

"I ... did." She was right, that it had happened. I didn't think this event truly had any bearing on my life, or anything to do with me in general, but it seemed important to Logan that it say something about me.

"Oh my God, Josie!" she said, and burst out laughing. There was nothing to do but wait until she finished.

Logan's skill in teasing was one of the social graces that served her very well, and I think it was one of the keys to her success in

Wells. In groups, she united us all against the person who revealed that they enjoyed watching *Desperate Housewives* or something similarly frivolous, or whoever was wearing the lamest shirt by her estimation, or whoever mispronounced a big word. You only had to pray it wouldn't be you. This ability, I was certain, was responsible for the inroads she had made with so many people in such a short amount of time.

I told Logan that I envied this about her. She did not acknowledge it as an ability as such, and it felt somewhat slimy to describe being likeable as a skill anyway. Nonetheless, this was how I thought about it. The only question was whether it was something one could learn.

In my experience, people generally decided if they liked you within a few minutes, and for me it appeared to be mostly random, because I didn't have any handy social tricks that charmed people like Logan did.

"I make friends with lots of guys, but I've never been popular with men. They always friendzone me," said Logan. I didn't understand how she could say this, because she had a boyfriend who liked her enough to agree to be long distance with her for a whole year. "You're probably much better with men than you think you are," she said. "You're actually attractive, you know." I thought that compliment might carry me through the entire year.

To my surprise, Brandon hadn't given up on me yet, and he seemed to still like me even though Logan was around. He invited me out to breakfast one morning. He sat us in a private corner of the pub and stared at me in a way I found intense. He kept taking off his glasses and rubbing them thoughtfully, as if he was preparing to say something important to me. When he started speaking I realized he actually just wanted to talk about Elon Musk.

"I think Elon Musk is an asshole," I said, trying to remember everything I knew about Elon Musk.

"How can you say that?! He's doing amazing things. You know he's developing a power system that actually saves power during the day? He's going to save the world."

"But he's a billionaire. Also, he seems like he's an asshole, especially to his wives."

"Pffft," said Brandon, "I once saw an interview with him and his girlfriend, that model —"

"Talulah Riley."

"Yeah, sure. He kept trying to talk to her, and she kept blowing him off. I think those women are using him for his money."

"That doesn't make it okay to be a billionaire," I said.

"Money doesn't really matter. I have thirty thousand dollars in student loans, but I'm not worried about it. I think Elon Musk doesn't think about money like other people."

In general, I liked it when men had glasses. I wasn't sure why. Maybe it was because my mother had had glasses when I was growing up. I thought it might be because it indicated a flaw, placing him more on my level, made him less frightening.

In any case, something about Brandon's glasses wasn't working for me. Perhaps it was the way they magnified his eyes, or that they were round like his face. Or maybe it was because he loved Elon Musk so much.

"What would you say your type is?" I asked Brandon, feeling bold.

"Oh, I think I like girls with short dirty blond hair, who don't wear too much makeup, and who are feminine, but not overly so," he said, describing my overall appearance. My ears rang for a minute, and I was struck with a strong desire to lie down on the floor. I chugged my water instead.

When I got home, Logan was out walking Oksana's dog. She had tracked her down when she learned she owned a big German shepherd and begged to be involved in its life. Only Hannah was home, and I found her in the kitchen.

"What's up?" she said. I told her what Brandon had said about his type, hoping she would offer me some clarity about the situation and what I might do about it. "Oh, that's so weird, that's exactly what I look like," she said. I went to my room and lay on my bed in the dark.

• • •

The next week, Brandon invited me to his apartment to watch television. He made us popcorn and poured melted butter on it. Half an hour in, I realized I had kept my coat on.

I didn't want him to kiss me, and I thought about how most of the time, when you hear about men and women spending time together alone, they end up kissing and sometimes having sex. It seemed impossible that that could happen to me and Brandon. No matter how many times I imagined it, there was no course of action I could think of that would end with us naked, in each other's arms. I had never had sex before, but I lied and told people I had whenever it came up because I knew that most people had had sex by my age. I made up various scenarios and guys, always emphasizing that I'd only done it once or twice to ensure I was being as emotionally honest as possible, despite the lie. I wasn't sure how I felt about Brandon, but I had a hard time imagining myself losing my virginity to him.

We watched *The Haunting of Hill House*. I pretended to be too scared to watch episode two and used this as an excuse to leave. As I stepped into the night, I wondered if anyone would see me from their windows and conclude that Brandon and I were sleeping together. This idea gave me a jolt in my stomach, and I found myself breaking into a canter, eager to get back home.

At therapy, I shared everything that had happened that week and my feelings about it as best I could with Barb.

"I'm still not even sure he is trying to hook up with me anyway," I said. "I don't know why he would."

"Um, he definitely is," said Barb, who sounded, for the first time since meeting her, a little bit annoyed. "He invited you to his house, he said you were his type. He obviously likes you."

"Maybe he was lying about me being his type."

"Why would he do that?" said Barb, looking like she was prepared to throw her little notebook on the ground.

"Because he wants to make me like him so he can feel like he has power over me."

"Do you think that's something that people do a lot?"

I shrugged.

"Let's say Brandon is telling the truth. Do you like him back, Josie?"

"I don't know," I said. "He likes me."

"But do you want to date him? Do you want him to kiss you? Do you like the idea of having sex with him?"

"I'm not sure."

"It's important for you to understand what you want. Every experience you have with other people can give you data about what you like and what you don't like."

"Hmmm."

"Every experience you have brings you closer to the reality you want, because you're learning each time. Does that make sense?"

"I guess so." I had never thought about life in quite that way before.

• • •

I considered Barb's advice carefully. All week, when anyone mentioned their physical bodies or things like giving blood, getting their period, or having sex, I grew nervous and faint, and excused myself from the room. I couldn't figure out what was wrong with me.

I understood my feelings better after Armand took Hannah out for dinner later in the week. I caught a glimpse of them as he was saying goodnight to her, preparing to take the long drive back to Quesnel, where his two teenage children were waiting for him. Hannah did not kiss or even touch Armand, who glared solemnly down at her like he was her security detail.

When Armand was gone Hannah joined Logan and me in the living room. Logan and I were always asking questions to try to get Hannah to reveal something about her relationship with Armand to us.

"Did you have fun?" Logan asked.

Hannah made an ambiguous noise. "I mean … it seems like he really likes me." She shrugged and smiled, bringing her hand to her lips as if deep in thought.

"Do you like him?" I asked.

"Well, he's old enough to be my father."

I couldn't think of a way to point out that she had not answered my question that wasn't aggressive. "What do you two talk about?" I asked. She told me that Armand was a farmer, and so he mostly described his work to her.

"You don't talk about anything else?"

She shrugged again and went to make nachos.

That evening, I sent Brandon a Facebook message: "Hey Brandon, I just wanted to check in with you because I've been thinking a lot about people leading other people on. Do you feel like I've been doing that to you?"

In the morning, I received a reply: "Hey Josie, no I definitely don't feel that way. I guess I do have a bit of a crush, but I definitely don't think you're stringing me along."

"That's good, because I don't think I feel that way about you. I'm glad we're friends, though."

"I hear you loud and clear. I'm glad we're friends too ☺"

As soon as I got this final message, I felt stupid. Someone had wanted to give me something, and I had rejected it. Brandon would never pursue me again. The relief I was experiencing was nothing, and my dread surrounding my interactions with Brandon was replaced quickly by yearning for the times we had spent together. I wanted to message him back, and tell him I was wrong, that I loved him and wanted to marry him. But I knew I wasn't supposed to do that.

I told Logan about the exchange. She was shocked that I would send a message like that.

"Wow, that is so forward, good for you!" she said. She sounded very impressed, as if I had just done a backflip or made her a perfect French omelette.

• • •

"I'm proud of you," Barb said when I told her what I'd done at our next session. "Even though it was hard for you, you did something that aligned with your values and what you really wanted, not what you thought you were supposed to want. Do you feel relieved?"

"No, I feel like a bitch."

"Because you rejected him?"

"Yes, and because I didn't see his value. Who am I to turn away a perfectly good man? What if I'm just a bad judge of character?"

"It doesn't matter, though," said Barb, "because you don't want to date Brandon, and that's fine."

"Okay," I said. "I don't think any man will express interest in dating me ever again."

"You might be surprised. You're still young, you know, Josie."

I replied with a noise that sounded like *huhhnn*.

Chapter 6

HANNAH WAS ALWAYS TRYING TO GET ME AND LOGAN TO join the volunteer fire department. As the chief, she ran fire practice every Thursday night from seven thirty until nine thirty.

"Wanna join? It's pretty fun," she'd say each week, poking her head into the living room to find Logan and me sprawled on the couch, preparing to begin some rom-com or erotic thriller.

"Mmmm, maybe next week?" one of us would say, rubbing our eyes, feigning crippling sleepiness.

Hannah was not asking us to come because she particularly liked us and thought we would be effective firefighters. Rather, she asked everyone to join whenever it was possible to slip it into conversation, like when someone mentioned free time or enjoying team activities, like a tactful youth pastor. She wanted to build a robust army of emergency personnel in Wells, at the ready to defend against chimney fires, of which there was at least one each winter on account of the widespread use of wood-burning ovens.

I did not like the idea of being a volunteer firefighter. The idea of attending fire practice evoked memories of soccer practice when I was a child, where I would do my best to listen and participate, and then find myself sitting in the grass, picking at dandelions and making up stories about *The Lord of the Rings* in my head in the middle of the semi-finals.

"I feel like it would be disingenuous to join the fire department. I'd only be doing it to tell people that I was a volunteer firefighter and to put photos of myself in the gear on Instagram and dating apps," I confessed to Logan. "I think I'd actually find it pretty boring."

"What?" said Logan. "You're so random, Josie!"

Being lazy people, Logan and I held out on joining the fire department for some time, preferring our evenings on the couch with a book or TV series and hot chocolate made with whole milk. However, by the end of November, it was clear that Wells was slipping deeper and deeper into an inescapable hibernation. With no Brandon calling on me, and our social calendars all but empty as temperatures outside dipped below minus ten and the snow banks piled higher and higher, we found ourselves seeking any excuse to leave the house. Following a discussion on our weekly trip to Quesnel, we agreed to tell Hannah that we would try out practice and become members of the fire department.

• • •

I loved the fire hall more than I loved most of the buildings in Wells. It was big and imposing, with an almost perfectly cubic body and red trim that reminded me of a Richard Scarry illustration. At the peak of the A-frame roof was a beautiful little steeple where the alarm lived. I had no way of substantiating this, but I believed that it was probably very good for your brain to see beautiful buildings and landscapes a lot. For this, I was happy that I lived in Wells.

Inside, it smelled like a community ice rink. Three charming red fire trucks sat waiting in the garage. Logan and I, along with a slew of other locals — including Jeremy, who was the deputy fire chief, Ivan the blacksmith, and Janine, who welcomed us both with hearty claps on the back — were instructed by Hannah to change into fire gear as fast as possible. I was handed a set of stinky gear that was slightly too big for me. We pulled on the fireproof socks and overalls. Jeremy stripped down to his underwear before putting his gear on.

"It's better for insulation," he said, shrugging.

Hannah instructed us all to climb into the biggest firetruck, which Janine then drove around Wells. Our task was to identify the twenty-five fire hydrants around Wells. This exercise, Jeremy explained, was like learning scales on an instrument — it taught your fingers where to go when you struck the keys during a song. If we spotted the hydrants every week, we would not have to think about where the nearest fire hydrant was in the event of a fire, but would know it instinctually.

Driving around Wells at night in the fire trucks was surreal. The cold and expansive white light of the trucks reached even small nooks and crannies in the surrounding flora, and cast an eerie glow into the nighttime that a car never could. The trees and shrubs, and the swamp bordering the wilderness just beyond the borders of town, appeared fragile somehow, as if only *just* keeping the untethered growth of nature out. The light, which starkly revealed the subtle movements of the plants and bugs, the wind and animals, made me feel like I was seeing something that was meant to be private. Like the natural world was doing unconscious work that humans were not supposed to know about, and I was spying on it.

Hannah wasn't sure what exactly we should do for the rest of the practice, and there was a moment where we all stood around in a group, waiting for her to make a decision.

"Are you kidding me?" Logan muttered to me under her breath. "I thought she did this every week?"

I also thought it was odd that she hadn't made a plan, but this struck me as the type of thing I would do. In my final year at university I ran for, and eventually won, the history student's association presidency, even though I knew very little about what it would entail, and if I was honest with myself I had little genuine interest in the position. The meetings I ran with the rest of the team were short, and disorganized, and a few times I forgot to show up altogether. In taking the role, my main motive was to pursue something outside of myself to create and demonstrate my value, my validity, because I hadn't been able to find it internally. Maybe, I thought, that's what Hannah was doing.

Eventually, she had us extend the ladders to practise climbing outside of the hall. There wasn't time for everyone to try, so Jeremy and Logan, the boldest among us, volunteered to go up.

I sat at the bottom of the truck with Eddie, a young man who looked about twenty and who worked as a custodian. He was known around town to have a penchant for wearing pocket watches and fedoras. Our job was to make sure that the ladder didn't shake while Jeremy and Logan were up there.

"Honestly, that's nothing," Eddie said to me, gesturing to Logan, fifty feet above us.

"Huh?"

"I've climbed way higher buildings than this! With no carabiners either."

"Oh?" I said. I was excited that Eddie was confiding in me, and I didn't even have to do anything to make it happen.

"I was climbing buildings twice this height when I was in high school." He explained to me that he used to be a free climber, and would climb the few skyscrapers in Edmonton.

"Why did you stop?" I asked.

"Because you can't risk your life all the time when you're a politician," he said seriously. He then revealed that he was, among other things, a recently elected Wells town councillor, as well as an aspiring chess grandmaster.

"Oh, my," I said.

When fire practice was over, we all changed into our regular clothes. Eddie placed his fedora back on his head. We went up into the loft above the garage and were each allowed to select a soft drink from a minifridge as a token of our efforts to keep the public safe from fires. Logan made a joke at Jeremy's expense about his underwear, and everyone laughed. In the bathroom mirror, I saw that my cheeks were red like they were sunburned. My limbs were deliciously tired even though I didn't think I had even moved that much. A pleasant fatigue washed over me as I sat in the loft, trying to think of clever things to say. It was wonderful to experience exhaustion as a by-product of something useful.

After I arrived home, I tried to write down how the light on the trees made me feel in the fire truck, about how it felt confusing and wrong but also beautiful. I did this for an hour before I realized it was midnight, and I had to go to bed. The effort of writing made my face oily, and when I woke up the next morning I had a new zit in the crevasse of my nose. I opened my laptop and read what I had written, which sounded horrible in the light of the morning. As much as I'd tried, my feelings were poorly expressed.

• • •

Winter arrived in full force when a snowstorm blew through town, leaving a twelve-hour power outage in its wake. We were sent home from work, and Hannah, Logan, and I huddled under blankets in the living room. Hannah was well accustomed to these issues and found it dull and inconvenient, but I fantasized about eating cold beans for dinner before the power came back on.

In town, I bought a pair of boots for $75. They were red, with funky patterns along the ankle, and had little flaps on the soles that, when flipped, revealed cleat-like spikes for extra snowy walks.

This time of year was striking because the snow was so new and completely white. Looking at it blinded you and made dark spots appear before your eyes when you went inside. Logan and I would jump in snowbanks on our way home from the pub.

The wintriness made me feel like climate change, which gripped me with unspeakable terror when I lived in the city, wasn't even real. How could it be, when I had seen a herd of caribou twice on different trips to Quesnel? I gave myself permission to forget about it.

Inspired by the dumping of snow, Logan and I conspired to become outdoorswomen. At the pub, we listed off things we would do together.

"We can get ski passes. They're about $200, but we'll use them so much they'll more than pay for themselves!"

"And snowshoes!"

"Maybe cross-country skis?"

We went on a hike through the back woods from Wells to Barkerville one Monday. We got lost, following the wrong path and realizing that we were on a trail left by a lone Ski-Dooer. We wandered around for two hours as the sun sank low in the afternoon, pretending to be relaxed and having a good time.

"Do you think we'll die out here?" I asked Logan when I couldn't take it anymore.

"Josie!" she said. "Obviously not! We're fine." Her teeth began to chatter.

"What if we meet a moose?" I asked, thinking of the story Rhoda had told me last week about her ex-neighbour Larissa, whose car roof had been torn off by an angry moose. Rhoda always told stories like this with a severe expression, like I was considering letting a moose tear the roof off of my car and it was her job to convince me otherwise.

"We're not going to meet a moose." Logan shivered.

We reached Barkerville at 5:00 p.m. The sun had long set, and it was desperately cold. I could have cried when I saw the soft lights illuminating Billy Barker's face — if the frozen air hadn't made tears physiologically impossible.

We ran as fast as we could down the highway. Inside, most of the personnel had packed up and gone home for the evening at four thirty, leaving only Sharon, who was catching up on some work.

"Well look what the cat dragged in," she said dryly, but with a smile. We told her about our hike, and that we'd gotten lost. She invited us to sit in the staff kitchen and wait for Ricky to finish his work in the park before giving us a ride home. We made endless cups of tea, none of which managed to warm us up quite enough. I kept touching my face, which was so cold that it felt like it belonged to someone else.

After we got home, we went to the pub and I ordered a poutine and sticky toffee pudding for dessert. Logan had an enormous burger. We ate in silence, occasionally making eye contact and smiling at each other. If anyone approached us, I let Logan tell the story of what had happened, each time altering the timing and pacing a little bit to maximize its entertainment value.

Somehow, outdoor activities weren't quite as appealing after that, and Logan and I spent much of the winter inside.

• • •

Through most of December, Wells was silent as the grave. Smoke poured out of the chimneys, connected to the wood-burning stoves in almost everyone's homes. The sides of people's houses were piled high with dry firewood covered in tarps, which made for quaint Instagram posts.

The sun set before four o'clock each day. I was sluggish and cold all the time, and I started to routinely crave the steak sandwich from the pub — its simplicity and its heartiness. So many people were gone, even people who said they were going to stay the whole winter. All of a sudden, I was the possibly youngest adult in town.

At fire practice, we used the ladders to put up Christmas lights on the fire hall and on the big fir tree across from the pub. Everyone came out and brought their children to watch. I was proud, even if I was just standing at the bottom beside the truck drinking hot chocolate.

Logan spent a lot of time in her room on the phone with Matt, and sometimes came out looking sad.

"God, I can't wait to get out of here!" she'd say, slumping beside me on the couch.

"Really?"

"Oh my God, yeah! I miss Vancouver, I miss the city! Don't you miss, like, going to clubs and hanging out with your friends?"

"Oh, yeah I do miss that." I didn't tell her that she was probably my closest friend in the world at that point. "Don't you like how … quiet it is, though?"

"Yeah, whatever. I'd rather dance!" She began disco dancing.

We got free memberships to the Wells gym through the fire department. The gym was a room in the basement of the school with two working treadmills and two broken treadmills, dumbbells, a variety of mats, and some weight machines. To pass time in the evenings, we would get DVDs from the library and play them on a teensy TV that was drilled into the gym wall, and we'd walk on the two treadmills side by side, putting on the subtitles so that we could understand what the actors were saying over the hum of the machines.

A big part of living in Wells in the winter was what might be called "board game culture." Janine invited me and the other staff house residents as well as Brandon and Hunter over for "games night." We were going to play something called Dominion, a game I had never heard of, but Logan had, and she was over the moon.

"You'll love it," she said.

She was wrong, though. She only thought I would love it because she loved it. I had never liked board games, and I felt guilty about this because I knew they were generally considered to be an anti-social thing to dislike. But that didn't make it less true.

I didn't like board games because they hindered true sociability. I didn't like having to focus on strategy, or winning or losing, when I actually just wanted to look someone in the face and tell them what I was thinking about. As a child I was always getting into fights with my friends because they wanted to play soccer, or chase boys, and I just wanted to walk around the soccer field and discuss matters, things I can't even remember now, but which needed to be parsed out verbally, without distraction.

In university I was able to plausibly defend my lack of interest in board games by criticizing the men who loved them as needing an activity in order to experience intimacy with each other. But by twenty-four, I didn't think that's what was going on at all, and the truth was that I simply wasn't raised to be competitive. I didn't want to win, I wanted to let someone else win so that they would like me. If someone tried to beat me at a board game or cards, I was confused. Why would someone use something so stupid to make themselves seem better than me? I would have done anything anyone wanted if they asked me to, including lose a board game, if it meant they'd think well of me.

Janine had a cottage just steps away from the staff house. It looked more like a magazine's rendering of a luxury cabin in the woods than any real cottage I had ever been in. The logs lining the exterior were laminated, the floors were heated, and one of the walls was outfitted with a flatscreen TV.

When Logan, Hannah, and I met Janine at her home along with Brandon and Hunter to play Dominion, she wrapped me in an enormous hug, before pulling away abruptly.

"Oops. I forgot, you don't like physical touch." I opened my mouth to explain that I didn't dislike physical touch necessarily, but it all felt a little bit too nuanced to put into words just then. I thought maybe Janine preferred to think of me as someone who didn't like to be touched. After all, sometimes I liked to think of people as very different from me to make myself feel more special, and I ignored evidence to the contrary. Janine hugged everyone else and didn't comment on their preferences for it.

Janine didn't act self-conscious around Hannah, despite Hannah's continued relationship with Armand. Brandon was still friendly to me, too. He seemed unfazed about the end of our short courtship; he acted normal. All of this made me feel crazy. How did people just walk around acting well-adjusted all the time?

Whenever I'd been rejected romantically in the past, it had made me want to act in ridiculous ways, and sometimes I did. After developing a particularly intense crush on a boy in my first year of university, I'd cried at every party I saw him at for the next two years. When I read *Anna Karenina*, it made perfect sense to me that a doctor thought Kitty might die after Vronsky rejected her, not even from heartbreak but from embarrassment.

That night I realized that Janine's favourite joke was doing a "gay man" voice, pretending to have a lisp and saying things like "faaaaaabulous." She did this a lot while we played Dominion, encouraging all of us to join in. Hannah was happy to tell us about how people often think she's a lesbian, but she's not.

"I don't really think it's nice to do a voice like that," I said to Janine. The table, once uproarious, became silent.

"What? What do you mean?"

"I don't think it's nice to make fun of gay men. Is the joke about them sounding feminine?"

"I'm not making fun of anyone," said Janine, very seriously. "I do this all the time with my gay friends in Vancouver — they love it. Besides, I'm bi."

"Oh," I said. Hannah and Hunter shifted uncomfortably in their sears, while Logan's face was lit up, like she was watching a parade go by.

"But, I get it," Janine said, her face jovial again. "It's a generational thing. If it bothers you, I won't do it anymore."

"Okay, thanks," I said. I hated to think that my problem was that I was from a different generation, and that it meant I couldn't be right, or that there was no right answer. Wasn't calling someone out for doing something you thought was shitty supposed to make you feel powerful? Wasn't that why people were always doing it on Twitter? I felt less powerful, and more confused. How were you supposed to know what it means to be a good person if everyone's idea of what "good" means is different? How was I supposed to impose it on others?

"Oh, how faaaaaabulous, sister. Oops, sorry, Josie," Janine said just a moment later as she was collecting a rare card from the deck.

The next week, we all went to board game night at the pub to play Trivial Pursuit. Hannah brought Armand, whose face and body language strongly suggested that he had not been expecting to spend the night at the pub with a bunch of Wells locals and his girlfriend's roommates.

Logan read out a science and technology question to Armand: "On October 4, 1957, what satellite was launched, becoming the first man-made satellite to officially orbit the Earth?"

"What does that have to do with science?"

"Well, a satellite is technology ..." Logan said. Armand sighed deeply and crossed his arms. After the first round he refused to play anymore, and instead whispered answers in Hannah's ear when she was unsure. Logan took issue with this.

"It's cheating!" she whispered to me. Just then, I was sort of grateful that I wasn't competitive.

Eddie and his girlfriend, Helen, who wore cat ears and often dyed the tips of her long hair different colours, sat a table over and played Scrabble together.

Helen turned to Logan and me. "I'm an English major, so I usually win." She rolled her eyes and grinned unselfconsciously.

I had never considered that being an English major could make you good at Scrabble. I thought it was more likely the other way around, that you'd become an English major if you had a natural predilection for word games. In any case, I was both bad at Scrabble and a former undergrad English major.

"They're soooo weird," Logan whispered to me.

They were, in truth, pretty weird, but I thought it was sweet when Eddie lifted his fedora slightly and leaned in to kiss Helen, planting his tiny kisses on her cheeks and forehead before landing tenderly on her mouth. I could call them weird all I wanted; I didn't have anyone to do that to me.

. . .

Christmas was fast approaching. This time of year was a big deal in Wells. Boughs of holly and fir trees, snowflake and snowman decals, and Christmas lights arranged in surprising ways appeared in town abruptly, decorating lawns, windows, and doorframes. Barkerville opened for one weekend for "Victorian Christmas," where the few interpreters left in town year-round dressed in their warmest period costumes and roamed the streets, greeting guests and serving hot chocolate.

The gold mine hosted an enormous, extravagant Christmas banquet at the town hall, reminding us all that their deep pockets and exploitation of the land were almost entirely responsible for keeping the Wells economy and the residents' crunchy granola lifestyles afloat. There was a ham, a turkey, and an unexpected lobster station, along with an obnoxiously diverse assortment of decadent sides and desserts. As we'd done for the chili cook-off, we all shoved Tupperware in our bags before we went, filling them to the brim by the end of the night. If locals were at all conflicted by the mine's presence in Wells and its involvement in the community, this dinner certainly quieted their concerns at least for the Christmas season.

Santa was portrayed by Martin, a long-time resident who interpreted Barkerville's own Billy Barker in the summer. He had a long, spindly white beard and seemed a little too small for the Santa suit. Children and a few cheeky adults approached him to sit on his lap and receive a present that the mine had paid for.

At the December cabaret, Jeremy performed a positively filthy poem about having sex with Mrs. Claus, adding a Santa hat to his scant ensemble. Charles got emotional, telling a story about breaking his leg and being invited to a Christmas dinner with other members of the community. Then he sang a song about Christmas that was from *Star Trek*. I averted my eyes as he sang, embarrassed.

He finished by saying that Wells was a place where everyone was welcome, and no one would be turned away. He received a standing ovation. Peering around, I saw that Brandon had big, fat tears welling in his eyes. In fact, almost everyone was smiling warmly up at Charles, many of them misty eyed.

It wasn't that I thought I wouldn't be invited to Christmas dinner by the good people of Wells if I didn't have anywhere to go. It was more that I knew the invitation would be out of pity, or duty, rather than any sense of closeness. Everyone liked Charles a lot, so of course, he would be welcome at Christmas dinner. I was reminded of high school, when the prettiest, most desirable girls would declare that their grade didn't really have a "popular group." I didn't know why everyone liked denying their power so much, but I wasn't sure I would have behaved any differently in their shoes.

Watching what was happening around me, I had a hard time picturing myself enjoying a merry Christmas with Janine, or Hunter, or Charles.

I had been in Wells for almost three months, and yet I was still sitting on the surface of a community. I was impatient to be loved, and terrified of the possibility that I would not be embraced after enough time had passed. I was torn between envy and resentment of the relationships I saw around me: Janine and Hannah, Hunter and Brandon, Logan and Jeremy, Hannah and Jeremy, Janine and Brandon, Sharon and Ricky. These feelings were punctuated by a sharp stick of guilt telling me I was rotten for being so entitled. *No one owes you anything*, it said. *You are not inherently lovable, you have to earn it. Besides, isn't what you have enough?* Perhaps my wanting so much is what prevented people from getting to close me.

Chapter 7

I TRAVELLED HOME FOR CHRISTMAS AND NEW YEAR'S. Ontario was green and dull compared to the bright snowy landscapes of northern B.C. Even the sun was different, mellow and lazy and in the sky much longer throughout the day. When I went outside, I got sweaty in my winter coat. Recalling where I had just been was discombobulating, like I had come from an entirely different planet.

My brother, a very insightful person, noticed a shift in me as well. "You're different now," he said, his expression grave.

"Different how?" I asked, intrigued to know how my time away had changed me.

He thought for a minute. "Your laugh is different," he said. "It's, like, sillier. It sounds like a baby."

"Oh."

While I was home, Eddie sent me a deposit of memes on Facebook Messenger. Four of them were about chess, and two were making fun of Justin Trudeau. I didn't have any specific reaction to any of the images and I didn't actually understand many of them. I responded "LOL!!!!!!" Eddie sent back a crying laughing face.

Every day that week, my siblings and I laughed a lot together, eating chocolates from our stockings and watching movie after movie in the afternoons before falling into decadent naps. I experienced an enormous pang of sadness when it was time to leave for the airport. It had been so easy to be home, my trip so full of happiness. For a minute, nothing about the Cariboo seemed exciting, or kind. I blinked back tears as I said goodbye to my parents.

· · ·

I flew into a massive snowstorm in Prince George. In the snow-blinding parking lot, my car was buried under what appeared to be an impossible amount of snow and ice. I had to dig with my arms to get into the back seat where the shovel and scraper were.

The roads were too bad to drive, so I checked myself into a hotel in downtown Prince George. I realized I was okay with this, and not in any real rush to get back to Wells, which made me depressed. After all, Logan was still home with her family, and Hannah probably wouldn't be excited to see me.

Sitting in silence on the bed in the hotel room, greasy and disoriented from travel, I wanted to turn this experience into a story that I could tell someone and make them laugh, but I couldn't think of who to call. Hadn't I met so many people over the years, people I had been close to at one time or another? Where had they gone? Was I so unpleasant or unremarkable that none of my friendships could survive distance and time? I was always moving away from people, first to Montreal for school, then to England, then to

B.C. Was I just waiting for someone to ask me to stick around, to be told that I was important to someone?

I typed out an account of my day in Google Docs, but when I read it back it sounded trivial and unworthy of documentation.

I ordered room service and watched the remake of *Sabrina* with Harrison Ford and Julia Ormond.

In the morning, my arms sore from all the shovelling in the airport parking lot, I wasn't sad. *At least Eddie sent me some memes*, I thought, checking Facebook. *Someone wants to talk to me.* It was a new year, after all.

I had my complimentary breakfast and left the hotel. The Cariboo was cold in a new way that morning. This was the dry cold that Hannah and Brandon and Vanessa were always talking about. When I breathed in the air, it made me cough, and a numbness crept over my face.

The drive was icier and more treacherous than it had been in December. The ice crunched noisily underneath my tires, and I had to turn my music up very loudly to drown it out. Occasionally, I passed a car in a ditch, intact but incapacitated, its driver standing forlorn beside it, shivering in the cold. I braced myself and went as slowly as I possibly could on the bends and curves of the gold rush trail into the mountains.

I was still delighted by northern B.C. It was as beautiful as ever, and I knew I was privileged to see it like this, when many people who could not withstand the climate had retreated to the south. Even the miners during the gold rush didn't typically stay the winter. I thought I was braving it swimmingly, like a true Wellsian. Didn't that stand for something?

On my drive, I considered the New Year's Resolutions that I had thought up during the plane ride the day before. My first resolution was to take up vegetarianism again, and my second was to be kinder to Hannah.

These were modest and manageable goals.

I turned my thoughts to the year ahead and wondered what would happen to me after March, when my internship ended. The future looked blank, like a black hole, as it so often did when there were no concrete plans. If there was no place that wanted me, it might be better to just disappear.

At the staff house, the door was unlocked but Hannah wasn't anywhere to be found. I hadn't gotten any groceries on the way back from the airport, so I went to the pub, carrying *Crime and Punishment* to occupy myself. I was dismayed to realize that the only item on the menu that was strictly vegetarian was the house salad. I asked Henrick for the rigatoni without sausage.

"What, you not eating meat or something?" said Rhoda, who was seated at the bar beside me with her husband.

"Oh, yeah, not right now," I said. "I don't eat a lot of meat anyway, so I decided to go vegetarian in the new year."

"What, you think meat makes you fat?" she asked.

"No, I don't think that."

"You scared of meat?"

"Not at all!"

Rhoda and her husband exchanged glances. "You know beef is really important for Alberta, where I'm from. If a whole bunch of youse decided not to eat it anymore we'd all be in a lot of trouble." She was laughing to herself, but seemed frustrated.

I didn't understand why I was being asked to defend myself. I had always thought people liked vegetarians. People were always saying things like "yeah, I should cut down on meat, too," and "good for you, I don't know how you do it!" to vegetarians in impressed and compensatory tones.

"It's just something I'm trying out," I said, shrugging, even though I wasn't really trying it out.

Rhoda exhaled and shook her head.

I turned my attention to *Crime and Punishment*. Logan had finished it before Christmas and had strongly recommended it. I opened to the first page and reread the opening paragraph over and over again. None of it made any sense to me. How had Logan managed to read this? It was so dense and confusing. Perhaps I was the stupidest girl in Wells.

My rigatoni arrived. As I stuck my fork in it, Rhoda turned to me again, apparently having taken some time to think about my situation.

"So, last week you did eat meat? And this week you're not?"

"Yup," I said. When she put it that way, it sounded so dumb. I suddenly felt extremely guilty that I had asked the kitchen to make an alteration to my meal.

"I just don't think that makes sense," she said. I put a bite of pasta in my mouth. It tasted good, but I couldn't help but wonder if it would have tasted better if there had been a big piece of spicy Italian sausage in it.

• • •

Hannah came home the next morning while I was preparing for work.

"Oh my God!" she exclaimed when she saw me. "I had no idea you'd be here!"

"Oh, sorry," I said, although I was quite certain that we had discussed the date of my return in detail over Facebook Messenger just two days before. Remembering my second resolution, I smiled widely at her. "Happy New Year, Hannah! How was your Christmas?"

"Ohhh, you know," she replied, now breezing past me to get to her bedroom.

It was just me and Hannah until the following Tuesday. Logan was still in Vancouver with Matt and her family and would be returning the following Monday. One quiet afternoon at the office,

Hannah asked if I'd like to make dinner with her, which made me wonder if her resolution was to be nicer to *me*.

"That would be wonderful," I said. "Do you mind if we do something vegetarian? One of my new year's resolutions is to stop eating meat for a bit."

"Oh," she said, sounding concerned. "Is something the matter?"

"No, everything's fine."

"Hmmm, well, I really, really wanted to make my orange chicken. It's a family recipe. I know some vegetarians eat chicken, would you eat that?"

"Um, no I don't think that would technically work," I said, having not heard of the phenomenon of vegetarians who eat chicken.

"Oh, that's too bad. Does it gross you out that I eat meat?"

"No, not at all. I just stopped eating meat this month."

"So, you were eating it last month, but you're not anymore?" Hannah said slowly, as if deciphering a slightly insulting riddle.

"If you really want to make orange chicken, I'll eat it, okay?" I said, finally.

"No, I don't want to make you uncomfortable."

I wanted to tell her that I was already uncomfortable, but remembered my resolution and kept my mouth shut. "Maybe we should just cook separately," I said.

"This is the worst," she said, hanging her head. "I *really* wanted to make dinner together."

I told Nancy about my new diet and the reactions I had been receiving. Since returning, Janine, Vanessa, and Melissa had all been exposed to my lifestyle change and had experienced various levels of confusion and frustration at my choice.

"I'm just not sure what's going on," I said. "People seem invested in my diet and are taking it very personally."

Nancy, ever the pragmatist, gazed at me from behind her hot pink glasses and shared some sage wisdom.

"In Wells, it's best to be flexible and not put too many labels on things like that, in case people have a lot of questions. Why do you *have* to call yourself a vegetarian, you know?" I found this advice difficult to swallow, because I thought I should be able to call myself whatever I wanted. But, considering who my neighbours were, I understood why she said it, and I vowed to be more careful when picking meat products out of my food.

For the new year, Nancy assigned me the task of reorganizing the archive room, getting rid of any redundancies in files, and removing duplicate documents. The archive room was frigid, and I tried to dress extra warmly on days I knew I'd be going in there, but no matter how many sweaters I wore, I felt my eyelids drooping each time I went in for more than fifteen minutes, like a lizard in winter. I'd let myself take long breaks and lie on the floor beside the stepladder. I was beginning to suspect that a life deep in the archives amongst temperature-controlled documents was not suitable for a person like me.

On Tuesday, I drove to Quesnel to pick up Logan, who was flying into the tiny local airport. On the drive down, it began to snow. It was the kind of snow that clumped together as it fell from the sky and made the world muffled and dream-like. It was very beautiful, but by the time I got down to Quesnel, my windshield wipers were on their highest setting and there was no sign of the snow letting up. I was inconvenienced, then impressed at myself for feeling inconvenienced by snow like an actual adult.

Logan walked from the little airport building to the car and was covered in wet, melty flakes. Some of them globbed onto me when she got in.

"Nice weather we're having, don't you think?" she said in a faux-British accent, gesturing to her wet exterior.

"Indeed, Logan."

"God, it's sooooo nasty up here! Did I have to come back to *this*?" She glared at the windshield, whose surface was now entirely engulfed in snow after five minutes in the parking lot.

"Yeah, it sucks," I said. "Glad you're back, though."

"I wish I could have stayed. It was so hard saying goodbye to Matt and all my friends."

"Yeah, same," I said. I knew that, legally, Logan was allowed to complain as much as she wanted about missing her boyfriend. But I envied her having a real life, with a boyfriend and people who wanted her around, back in Vancouver. She wasn't at all preoccupied with fitting in, or finding a home, let alone making one in Wells, because she already had one. I sometimes privately wished she didn't have a boyfriend so that we could be more on the same page in life and could make plans together without an expiration date.

Within the few minutes we were parked together at the airport, something had changed outside. I put the key in the ignition and shifted into drive, but the road below me felt different, my field of vision even more limited than before.

"Oh, my God," I said.

"Yikes," Logan said. "Want me to drive?"

"No, no, I think it's okay. Besides, you've had a long trip." Travelling just the length of road from the airport to the gold rush trail leading to Wells, which normally took ten minutes, now took almost thirty on account of the low visibility and the bumpy, slippery sensation beneath my tires that made me incredibly nervous. Before we knew it, night had fallen, and a barrage of logging trucks was barrelling toward us. Reckless in the best of driving conditions, these trucks seemed to have no regard for human life, and they happily met us with their most aggressive LED high beams.

"Jesus Christ, Jesus Christ," I said to myself over and over. I'd long since turned the music down, feeling that it somehow made my vision worse. I squinted at the road, trying to see as far ahead as possible, to anticipate any tricky turns that would not be obvious in the blizzard. Logan said something I couldn't hear.

"Hmmmm," I replied.

"Big moose," she said.

"What?"

"Big moose, big moose, Josie!" A pair of glowing yellow eyes came into focus. I slammed on the breaks and my car skidded gently but freely on the highway. In my effort to see into the distance, I had not been able to register the enormous moose I was fast approaching. I thought about Rhoda's ex-neighbour and the hood of her car.

The moose, perhaps also struggling with visibility, paid us little mind and went slowly across the road and into the forest. I wondered where moose went when it snowed like this, if they just had to stand in the middle of the forest somewhere, closing their eyes tight to avoid aggressive snowflakes getting in them. I was sorry for the moose then and grateful to be at least in a car with one layer of protection from the elements. We exhaled.

"Oh my God."

"Oh my God!"

"I am so ready for this car ride to be over," said Logan.

What was normally a fifty-five-minute drive turned into an immersive two-and-a-half-hour horror experience. Going only thirty kilometres per hour, blinded by the snow and confronted by loggers around every corner, Logan and I were dead quiet for most of the drive, not from any awkwardness or lulls in conversation but from deep concentration and dread.

We passed Devil's Canyon, the part of the drive with the steepest and most frightening drop-off into the chasms below, and the car began to spin out slowly, refusing to listen to my foot when I slammed on the breaks, going wherever it pleased.

"Fuckfuckfuckfuckfuck." For a moment, reality was skewed. Time was at a standstill, and I was aware of the danger I was in, and yet my body did not, or refused to, reflect this. I was calm as the car drifted, knowing that it would either stop, or continue to spin and move across the ice until it hit something or slid off the road and down the steep hills. *Okay*, my body seemed to think, *let's see what happens.*

After an indeterminate period of time, the car stopped spinning. It was freezing inside the car, but I was sweating.

We arrived at the staff house, exhausted and introspective.

"I think there was probably a fifty-fifty chance that we weren't going to make it," I admitted to Logan.

"I was going to say seventy-thirty," said Logan. We laughed. The next week, Logan and I decided to skip our trip to Quesnel for the first time since moving to Wells, having had quite enough excitement for one lifetime.

Chapter 8

THE SLOW AND STEADY RHYTHM OF LIFE PICKED BACK UP again smoothly: work, home, pub, fire practice, gym, Quesnel, Barb, groceries, books, movies, repeat. At our first fire practice of the new year, Hannah instructed us all on how to open a fire hydrant and attach the fire hose to it. Ivan, the blacksmith with stylish grey hair, helped me when I couldn't manage to open it. Watching his strong arms so easily turn the spoke made me really horny. I thought about it for the rest of the week, and about arms in general, and big strong shoulders, and attractive hair.

"Say, Josie, what's that buzzing sound I've been hearing in your room every night this week?" Logan asked me, feigning confusion, as Hannah drove us home from work one evening.

"Uhhh," I said, "it's ..."

"It's okay, Josie," Logan said, patting me on the shoulder.

"Um, am I missing something?" Hannah said.

"It's my vibrator," I said.

"Oh ..." Hannah said, her voice touched with alarm. "Where would you even buy something like that?"

"Seems like Josie has her ways." Logan was laughing.

"Well, everyone has their own likes and dislikes, I guess," said Hannah, as if sex itself were a fringe interest.

"I mean, c'mon, haven't either of you owned a vibrator?" I said.

"No, I could never go to a" — Hannah lowered her voice — "sex shop."

"I mean, I ordered mine online," I said.

"That's none of my business," she said.

"I have Matt," Logan said, shrugging. *Not right now you don't*, I wanted to say. I started using only my fingers to masturbate, but the damage was done. My sexual appetites became Logan's favourite talking point when the three of us were together.

. . .

Logan could judge my horniness, but she *was* missing Matt. In the evenings, she'd spend hours in her room on Skype, finding a movie on Netflix and pressing play at the same time, and emerging from her room misty eyed a few hours later.

After much pleading, he agreed to come see her for a few days. He was going to bring his friend Ruben. They spent the whole day driving from Vancouver, while Logan and I prepared the house. We were lucky, Logan said, because Hannah was out of town, visiting her parents with Armand.

"I doubt she'd tolerate their antics," Logan explained. "They can be a bit ... much when they're together."

Logan made a huge pot of chili for Matt and Ruben. "It's my famous recipe," she said. She was an unusual cook. Her recipes usually turned out tasting delicious, but I found I liked them better when I didn't know how she made them. I watched while she cooked, peering over her shoulder as she added ketchup, a can of salsa, and Worcestershire sauce to the pot.

"And chocolate!" she said proudly. "That's the secret ingredient."

We couldn't find any chocolate in the pantry, so we searched the house until we found a mini bag of M&Ms hidden amongst Hannah's piano music.

"Perfect!" said Logan, dropping them into the chili. We watched the coloured candy coating dissolve into the brown mush. I wondered how Logan's chili would fare against Lyle Smith's award-winning recipe.

I was nervous to have men in the house. Usually, when I tried to engage with a man and be his friend, I ended up regretting it. Not that I blamed them. By twenty-four, I was well aware that something about me just put men off. I thought it was probably either the quiet desperation that clouded all of my behaviours and interactions, or my massive calves.

"Ruben is such a great guy," said Logan as we cleaned a massive pile of Hannah's stuff out of the living room. "He's just like Barney from *How I Met Your Mother*! He gets with sooo many girls."

Hearing this made me uneasy. Would he try to sleep with me? I wasn't sure whether him trying to sleep with me would feel better or worse than him not trying to sleep with me.

At six thirty, Logan and I peeked out the window to watch for their car together, even though it was so quiet outside that we would certainly hear them pulling into our driveway. Outside, only the moon shone on the frozen piles of snow, which glistened softly. Logan and I feigned childish excitement in anticipation of their arrival.

Ruben and Matt appeared in the driveway around seven, and they knocked on the door in an overly aggressive fashion, I assumed as a joke.

"Matt!" Logan screeched, pulling it open. Matt whisked her up into his arms. This became awkward because she was so much taller than him. As he cradled her, her long legs almost reached the ceiling. Logan didn't care, and wrapped her arms around his neck, kissing his cheek.

Ruben, entering behind Matt, was very tall, and wore a grey hoodie and track pants and no coat.

He was about as tall as Logan, and he, too, lifted her into the air and spun her around. Matt hugged me. I panicked, and placed my hand on the small of his back as he did. Then, Ruben hugged me.

"I've heard *a lot* about you," he said pointedly. I furrowed my brow, trying to think of how to respond to this. Something told me I should say something flirty, but I couldn't think of anything.

"Well … all good stuff, I hope!"

Ruben watched my face intently as I said this, his expression warm. He was intense, but friendlier than I was expecting.

Once they'd brought all their stuff inside, Ruben dropped to the ground and began doing push-ups. Matt opened the cupboard to get a cup of water and found the Smirnoff Ice that Logan had hidden there.

"Fuuuuuck!" he said. He smashed the rim of the bottlecap against the counter, and got down on one knee, chugging. Logan put on "Party Rock Anthem." Ruben took off his hoodie, revealing chiselled abs underneath. Logan and I opened beers for one another, and she poured Matt a whisky. As Ruben resumed his push-ups, and Matt and Logan began to make out, I was relieved that Hannah was away.

• • •

Logan was eager to serve Matt her chili.

"It's my famous recipe," she repeated. She had prepared him a bowl and added a dollop of sour cream and little chopped green onions, which I thought was very chic of her.

I made a bowl for myself and thought it tasted amazing. There was a certain M&M quality to it that would be difficult replicate in even the finest kitchens.

Matt took a bite and made a thoughtful face.

"It's not bad," he said, after a moment.

Logan was devastated. "Not bad?"

"Yeah, not bad," said Matt.

"How can you say that? You know it's great!"

"Don't be such a girl, Logan," said Matt. "You know I'm an honest guy. I'm not going to tell you it's amazing if I don't really feel that way about it."

She stood up and walked to the other side of the room, folding her arms. "Wow, Matt." He sighed deeply.

"Logan, this is just who I am, you gotta accept that I'm not someone who will ever tell someone I love something if I don't mean it, that's just not me. You have to respect that about me." He rose to follow her and wrapped his arms around her. She stiffened.

"I really like it!" I said, but no one heard me.

"Logan, I've known Matt since we were five," said Ruben, who was enjoying his chili immensely by the looks of it. "*Five.*" He repeated, as if it was a very significant number. "You have to accept him the way he is, he's not going to change. Really, what he said is a compliment, coming from him."

"That's true, that's true," said Matt, nodding seriously.

I didn't think Logan needed to accept this about Matt. He was being pretty annoying. But their voices were so confident, and they said it so many times, that I started to wonder if they were right. Eventually, Logan yielded to Matt's kisses and started laughing.

• • •

I ate two bowls of chili. After dinner, we played a drinking game where we laid a big sheet of paper out on the table and everyone wrote rules and instructions. We'd throw a bottle cap, and where it landed, we'd have to follow the instructions written there, like "sing a silly song," "remove one article of clothing," or "hands on your nose, last one drinks!"

Ten minutes in, I was doing a sexy dance in my bra. Logan had to shotgun two beers in a row. Then, Ruben had to kiss me.

I didn't really want to kiss Ruben, but I had to, because we were all supposed to be having fun and Ruben was making a face like he really wanted to kiss me. He placed his enormous hand on the back of my head and pulled my face to his. He began rhythmically moving his mouth on top of mine. I hadn't kissed anyone in a few years, and this re-introduction was slimy.

I moved to pull away, but Ruben held my head in place with his giant hand, letting his tongue explore my mouth. The movements and the sounds coming from his throat made me believe this was an exciting experience for him. I kept my face and mouth as still as possible.

When Ruben finally pulled away, he stared at me with an expression that I could tell he thought was sexy.

"That was … incredible," he said, still watching me. "Actually, your lips are very soft."

"Thank you," I said.

Eventually, it was Logan and Matt's turn to kiss, and my turn to kiss Logan, and Logan's turn to kiss Ruben, and my turn to kiss Matt. We exchanged chaste pecks.

"Awww," said Logan as my lips met Matt's.

I was quite drunk, but it didn't feel that way because Matt, Ruben, and Logan were much drunker than me. Ruben took a leftover pumpkin from Thanksgiving and smashed it on the ground outside, and we watched its rotted insides explode against the ice.

Back inside, Matt and Logan disappeared into her room. Ruben darted over to me. His eyes were half closed.

"Okay, we only have a few minutes," he said, and he drew me toward him, planting kisses on my face.

"What?" I said. He put his hand on my ass.

"Well, we can make out more, can't we?" he said, whispering into my face, his hot breath going into my eyes.

"Oh, I don't think I can right now," I said. He laughed and leaned in to kiss me. I put my hands on his chest and gently pushed him away, like I had seen Pam do to Jim in the season two finale of *The Office* when I was fourteen. He complied, and sat down on the kitchen floor.

"What's really interesting about you is, you're hot, but you're also kind of plain?" he said, leaning his head against a cupboard and closing his eyes. I thought he might fall asleep.

"Oh," I said. "Thanks."

Eventually, Logan and Matt reappeared, both in great moods. Ruben seemed to have recovered his energy, and the four of us went to the pub. Logan looked around the bar at the familiar patrons, beaming with drunken pride at her boyfriend.

We ordered tequila shots, and when I shook the salt onto my wrist, Ruben grabbed it and started to lick me.

"No, Ruben!" Logan said, yanking my hand back. "No!"

"Huh?" said Ruben, who seemed to have instantly forgotten what he'd just done. "Whassup?"

Logan pulled me aside. "Are you okay?" she asked.

"Oh, yeah!" I said. "Totally."

"I know Ruben can be kind of intense, I hope everything's okay."

"I think it's fine," I said. It wasn't clear what she meant by intense. Was she alluding to something? Or did she just mean he was intense?

When Ruben tried to climb onto the pool table, it became clear he was too drunk, so we all went home. I felt kind of bad, because I realized that no one had warned them about the blood oxygen levels. Matt was sleeping in Logan's room, and Ruben was going to sleep on the couch.

Safe in my room, I changed into my pyjamas. When I went to shut off the lights, I turned the lock on my door knob, then I crawled into bed, feeling ashamed of my paranoia.

I woke with a start some minutes later when the door handle began to rattle violently. I shot up. The door shook. The person on the other side was putting the weight of their body against it. I pulled my blanket up to my chin. Then came Ruben's voice: "Do you have weed?"

"No!" I said. "Goodnight!" The handle kept shaking, the door rattling in its frame. "I don't have weed!" I shouted again. The movement stopped, then started again, before everything was still and quiet. Somehow, I fell back to sleep.

The next day, Ruben and Matt went skiing and, despite their big night, were gone when I woke up. I found Logan in the kitchen, looking groggier than normal. She flashed me a sneaky smile as I sat down beside her.

"So, I hear you had a late-night visitor," she said.

"Yeah, Ruben was knocking on my door. He said he wanted weed." I had a headache.

"He said you locked your door!" said Logan. "You don't usually do that, do you? I didn't tell him that, of course." She added quickly.

I shrugged, feeling guilty. "Yeah, I guess I was just more comfortable that way."

"That's so funny!" she said.

"I guess so. I was worried that he was trying to get in to have sex with me," I said.

"Oh, he was. That's what he told me this morning."

"Oh."

"Oh my God, this is so funny. Ruben is so crazy!"

I scurried off to work while Logan took a day off and joined the boys at the hill later in the morning. That evening, I said I wasn't feeling well and declined to go to dinner, locking myself in my room again when I heard the door slam shut later in the evening. When it was time for them to go the next morning, I gave them warm hugs, and Ruben kissed me on the cheek.

"Till next time," he said, winking.

• • •

In town the next Tuesday, Barb was disturbed by what she heard.

"So, you'd never locked your door before, but you did it that night?" she asked.

"Yeah, I felt kind of stupid doing it. And I'm embarrassed that Logan thinks it's so funny."

"You shouldn't be," said Barb. "You followed your instincts, and they served you well."

"I dunno. I don't want to like, make myself into a victim, or assume that I would have been one, when nothing actually happened to me. Like, he'd only kissed me before then. I had no real reason to be afraid of like, sexual assault."

"But you were, weren't you?"

I wasn't sure whether I had been afraid. In my freshman year of university, one of the first times I had ever been drunk, a friend and I had knocked on the door of a boy I had a crush on in my residence after a party. When he opened the door, I collapsed in a pile at his feet, laughing uncontrollably. Later, I barfed into a plastic bag and cried for my mother while my roommate rubbed my back. My crush had been kind about the whole thing when I saw him the next day, but he did not want to date me. I was embarrassed, but that was it. Had he been afraid of me? The guilt I experienced when considering this was dizzying. Wouldn't I be a hypocrite to say I had been afraid?

• • •

At the end of January, it was my twenty-fifth birthday. Logan made me an enormous chocolate cake and we took it to the pub, where we passed out pieces to all the patrons who happened to be there. Henrick gave me a free drink, and Janine brought me two bars of chocolate, which touched me because I didn't think she liked me very much. I let her wrap her big arms around me and squish me into a hug. Everyone sang "Happy Birthday," and I wanted Henrick to put on ABBA, but Logan said they were too silly. Everyone was being so nice to me, but I couldn't tell if it was just because we had given them cake.

I stared at myself in the mirror in the pub bathroom and touched my cheeks and forehead, trying to find differences. I was exactly the same.

I was still flustered wherever I was, and I volleyed between loving and hating myself and everyone I knew, so sharply I sometimes got headaches trying to land somewhere. Embarrassment, envy, and shame all ran just as hot in my veins as they had the year before, with no end in sight. My emotions, and the point of my existence, remained a mystery to me. My purpose on Earth so far seemed to only be to want stuff and get mad when I didn't get it. When would this change, and how? Would I start getting things, or stop wanting them?

Eddie had still been sending me chess-related memes every week or so, and I had begun to internalize this as a regular part of my life. I was on the couch eating a bowl of chocolate chip cookie dough ice cream and staring at Ask Reddit when I got a Facebook Messenger notification from him.

"Good evening, Miss Josie!" Eddie wrote. This is what Eddie had begun calling me at fire practice and around town, even though he just called Logan "Logan." He even tipped his fedora to me sometimes.

"Hi Eddie, how are you today?" I replied.

"I'm just wonderful. I wanted to ask you, would you like to accompany me to this event next week?" He pasted a link. My stomach dropped as I opened it. I had heard of the event. A Vancouver chef was coming to the Jack to make a six-course meal on the weekend after Valentine's Day. The banner photo of the Facebook event was a picture of a bacon-wrapped scallop overlaid with little hearts.

"Oh, God," I said out loud.

"What is it?" said Logan, who sat reclined on the couch across from me, balancing a bowl of tortilla chips on her stomach.

"Eddie just asked me to go to this with him." I turned the computer to show her. She laughed out loud.

"Ooooooooooh, someone has a ca-rush on youuuuu." Sometimes Logan came to conclusions easily and quickly, without stopping to sift through all of the relevant information. To her, if you use a vibrator, you are a voracious nymphomaniac; if you put a whole can of coconut milk in your soup, then it's no longer healthy. I tried to make a face that would show her that I did not find this situation funny. She didn't notice. "Ooh ooh ooh," she sang.

"He has a girlfriend, though, right? Helen? What about her?" My voice was frantic.

"I thought so, too." Logan gazed up at me from under her eyelashes coyly. "Maybe he dumped her for you!"

"No! I feel like I saw them together last week. They're always kissing."

"You know what, Ricky did mention something about them fighting last month."

"Oh God, this is a disaster!"

"What! No, not at all. This event looks awesome! I wish I was going."

"Well, I can't go obviously!"

"Why not?"

"Because I don't like him!"

"You mean you don't find his fedoras sexy?"

"Oh God," I said.

"Listen, you can't reject him." She ate a chip.

"I can't? Isn't it the right thing to do?"

"No, if he is broken up with Helen it would devastate him. He's obviously kind of a, er, sensitive guy. If they're still together then he probably just wants to go as friends."

"Yeah. Yeah, you know what? Maybe I can just assume they're not broken up and that I think it's like a friend hang, right?"

"I mean, maybe. Seems like a date to me, though."

"Okay, okay. That's what I'm going to do," I said, ignoring this. I had a good feeling about this plan.

I typed my response: "Wow, thanks so much for the invitation. That sounds like fun, I'd be happy to join. Where can I buy tickets?"

"Excellent. And no need to worry about tickets, I already bought them."

"Oh, well let me know how much it was and I can reimburse you."

"Absolutely not," he wrote. "I invited you to the event. I would never let you pay."

"Oh no!" I said to Logan. "He paid for the tickets already and won't let me pay him back."

"Told you!" Logan said. "It's going to be *super* romantic."

"Isn't Eddie like twenty-one or something?" I said. "He's kind of young for me."

"Oh, I thought he was like eighteen," said Logan. "But Josie, love has no age."

"Oh, wow, thank you," I typed to Eddie, defeated. "That's so kind of you. I hope you'll change your mind, though."

"Not a chance. ;););)" he wrote.

"Oh well. It can't have been that expensive, can it?" I said to Logan.

"Think again." She was reading the event page on her phone. She showed it to me: "Tickets - $150."

It was all so surreal. Two men interested in me already this year? That had to be a record, I said to Logan.

"One of the benefits, or drawbacks, of being in a small town. Depends how you think about it, I guess. Besides, I think we could place Eddie under the *boy* category, rather than the *man* category, right?" she said.

I spent the week anticipating our date and all the ways it could possibly go. Over and over, I imagined sitting down with Eddie under the spotty overhead lighting of the Jack for the entire town to see, while the enormous and tacky Amun-Ra statue gazed down at us as if to say, *huh, I didn't think he was your type Josie!* Thinking about it made me sweat.

I had a dream about arriving at the Jack to find it had turned into a cathedral, where Eddie and Brandon fed me oatmeal from enormous spoons.

"I think it sounds exciting!" Barb said when I told her about it.

"I don't think it sounds exciting at all!" I said.

"Why not? It could be romantic, or at least fun."

"But Barb, he wears a fedora and little formal vests every day. How could I possibly go on a date with him? What will people think?"

"What will they think?" Barb asked, in the way therapists do when they're being both rhetorical and genuinely curious.

"Um, people will draw conclusions about my character based on my association with him," I said. "It'll be embarrassing."

"You seem very anxious about this date. You've been grabbing at your hair *a lot* today."

I dropped my hands into my lap. "That's because I am very anxious about this date," I said, not without petulance. "I don't want to go."

"Because you'd be embarrassed to be seen with him?"

"Because of ... the whole thing of it. I'll have to wear something nice, but I'll feel slutty if I look too nice. I always get diarrhea on dates and can never eat much because I'm scared I'll throw up, and then I end up missing out on amazing food. People will be watching."

"What would you do if you weren't nervous about ... all of this?"

"I'd probably go to be polite, but make it clear that I am not interested, and that this is a friendly date only. A one time thing," I said.

"Okay, so maybe this is a good opportunity for you to practise doing something that might be fun without worrying about what other people think?"

"I guess so. But it's not like it's going to be this perfect time. We're not going to fall in love or anything. Also, aren't I supposed to be honest with people about how I feel about them? What about Brandon, wasn't it good that I made up my mind about him?"

"That was good," said Barb. She gazed at her hands, a pensive expression on her face. "You know, Josie, I went through a pretty difficult divorce when I was pretty young."

"Oh?" I said, trying to sound sympathetic, but unsure of how this might relate to my situation.

"Yep. And after that happened, something changed for me. I realized that I had closed my heart." She brought a hand to her chest. "I think I had to do it to protect myself at the time. But eventually, I knew I had to get back out there again and take a chance on something. I started going on lots of dates, trying to move on and move forward with my life. I went on one date a week for a long time. But something wasn't right, it wasn't clicking."

"No?"

"No." She shook her head, smiling to herself. "I realized that my heart was still closed. I never opened it up again." She patted her hand over her heart again. "It took a long time, but eventually, I felt it open again. I mean, I really felt it open." She moved the hand as if opening a little door to her bosom. "I remember the exact moment, and who I was with when it happened. It hurt a little, and for a second I could hear it creak."

"You heard it creak?" I said.

"Yes, it was a little rusty, but it opened."

"Wow," I said. In many ways, Barb was a conventional therapist, and sometimes I thought her methods were too by the book, and that I could easily outmanoeuvre them, or I even worried that she didn't really even see me or understand the nuances that my stupid problems presented. But she was truly singular in that I could not imagine anyone else, let alone another therapist, describing how her heart was healed in magical realist terms to me with such earnestness.

I wanted to say, "That's beautiful, Barb, I love you, and sometimes I wish you were my mother." Instead, I said, "Was the person you were with wearing a fedora?" Barb laughed, which I thought was generous because I was undercutting her story with a joke. "Okay, Barb, I'll try to open my heart to this guy and his vests."

"Maybe you'll have a *wonderful* time," she said. "What if he turns out to be best the person you've ever met?"

"I guess that's possible," I said. Technically, she was right. Softened by Barb's story, I wondered if I was being too judgmental about poor Eddie and jumping to conclusions about his character and value. After all, he was interesting enough to have a lot of hobbies and a unique fashion sense, and at least he was ambitious and forward enough to ask me out, even if he did have a girlfriend already. Maybe Barb was right, maybe he was my true love.

For my diarrhea, Barb sent me to the health food store and instructed me to buy a supplement that cost $40.

• • •

The day of my date, I still had diarrhea, even though I took my expensive supplement every day for the rest of the week. For dinner, I wore a long dress with a sweater that I thought hid my body well enough. I wore brown eyeshadow, and then went back and forth about washing it off, eventually leaving it.

I was ready early and opted to head straight to the Jack, not wanting to sit on the couch with Logan and Hannah and listen to their jokes about my date.

The dining room was arranged with white tablecloths and black and white salt and pepper shakers, giving the room a disjointed but formal appearance. Millie Saunders, a Wells local and a high school senior, was the waitress.

"Um, are you here for the event?" she asked, smiling a big grin at me. She had layers of dark eyeliner encircling her light-blue eyes that made her seem exactly seventeen.

"Uh, yeah," I said, feelish skittish now that I had to admit it was all real.

"Wonderful!" she opened a binder and ran her finger down a list of names. "Um, I'm not seeing you ..." She squinted. "Oh!" she said, and an even bigger grin erupted across her skinny face. "Oh, are you with … Eddie?" She turned, silently signalling to the other waiter, a gothic person with spacers in their ears and salt-and-pepper hair. They exchanged what they clearly thought were inconspicuous glances.

"Um, yeah, I am." It sounded like an apology. I watched the floor.

"Oh! Oh, that's —" She paused. "That's … *great*! Let's get you to your table." She smiled to herself as I followed her to what appeared to be a makeshift seating area beside the drink cart. The table was much lower and wider than the others.

"Eddie *really* had to push to get this table," she said. "He used to work the bar here, so the owner did him a solid."

"What?"

"Enjoy your evening!" she said, cantering away.

I sat down, facing an unadorned wall. I thought about Barb, who was probably enjoying a nice, unembarrassing meal with her husband and not thinking about me at all.

The room began to fill up quickly. I spotted Janine, who approached me and squeezed my arm before announcing again that she had forgotten that I don't like touching.

"I don't mind touching, I swear it," I said. This narrative around physical contact that Janine was always compelling me to act out with her was slowly eroding my relationship with the truth of the matter. It was as if by reciting these lines over and over, she could make it true that I hated touching, or could unlock some secret, truer part of myself that hates touching that only Janine could see. "It's more that … I don't touch a lot of people."

"Huh," she said sadly. "Well, maybe someday you'll enjoy it more. You here alone?"

"Um, no I'm waiting for a friend." This was technically true.

"How mysterious! I have a friend up from Vancouver and I thought I'd show them a good time." She gestured to a table on the other, more populated side of the room. "Have a nice evening!" She turned and walked away.

"You, too."

I sat, silently facing the wall for a few more minutes before a voice announced itself behind me. "Good evening, Miss Josie." I turned to see Eddie in his most formal fedora, black with a peppermint trim. Instead of a vest, he wore matching suspenders.

"Hi, Eddie!" I said, very enthusiastically. I could sense that I was tapping into some reserve of poise that I must have been saving up for emergencies. I threw my arms around him in a perfectly warm but brief embrace like one would give to an old friend. I felt Eddie's arms grow tighter as I began to pull away, but through force of will I drew my body back and successfully ended the hug.

"You look beautiful tonight," Eddie said. I could not remember the last time a man had called me beautiful, and I thought this surely must count in Eddie's favour.

"Thanks, Eddie. You look nice, too." I listened hard for any creaking sounds coming from my heart area. It was silent.

Millie came back around to our table and was now more composed, probably on account of the onslaught of distracting guests she'd had to attend to.

"Can I get you both a drink to start?" I ordered white wine, and as Eddie placed his drink order, I gazed over at the Amun-Ra statue, who stared down on me inscrutably. What was he thinking?

Millie brought our drinks shortly, mine a big pour of sauvignon blanc, and Eddie's a mysterious creamy-white beverage in an old-fashioned glass. Eddie brought it to his lips and took a big sip.

"Ahhhhh!" he said.

"What is that?"

"This, Miss Josie, is a virgin White Russian."

"Oh … what's in that?"

Eddie grinned at me. "Well, it's a glass of milk."

"Oh!" I said. "Wow."

He took another big gulp.

I did my best to be a nice date. I smiled and thanked him when he told me he liked my blond hair and that physically I reminded him of Sabrina the Teenage Witch. I thought this was sweet, but I couldn't think of anyone he reminded me of who wasn't a Batman villain. He described to me his favourite anime, and explained how he was going to become the prime minister one day, and that he didn't think he needed to get a degree to do this.

"First step was Wells council," he said, making slow chopping movements to signify different stages of his plan. "Then next term I'll run for mayor. Then after my stint in municipal government I can move to provincial, then federal. People don't need all that nonsense they teach you at universities. It's half propaganda anyway. Everyone comes out brainwashed. You have to do your own research."

"Hmmm," I said. I had been to university twice, and I could not tell whether I was brainwashed or not. "I think universities encourage people to push the envelope and go further than their predecessors to create a better world," I said. "I think that's why sometimes ideas about how the world should be extend to a natural, progressive extreme there and conservatism is frowned upon."

"People need to understand that the world needs balance. Surely, the answer must lie somewhere in the middle of liberalism and conservatism."

I had heard this argument for centrism before, but to me it made no sense because it implied that the centre was fixed and universal. Surely we would not, and should not, have pursued a centrist approach to the German government in the Second World War, a defeat Eddie had expressed great reverence for on Remembrance Day? I opened my mouth to speak, but I realized that if I told him what I thought then he would tell me what he thought about what I had said, and it would go on and on, with no end in sight. I realized I was not interested in that at all. I did not think I could change

Eddie's mind, and I did not think he could change mine, or want him to. If he did, it would disturb me.

"Hmmm," I said instead. "Maybe you're right. I should probably read more about that." He drained the last of his virgin White Russian.

"You *definitely* should. I can recommend you some great books." I smiled.

Dinner was incredible. There was lots of meat, and I ate it all.

"I thought you were vegetarian these days?" said Eddie as I bit into a piece of rare steak smothered in herbed béarnaise.

"Yeah, whatever," I said. "I don't like to put too many labels on things." Eddie seemed very happy with this explanation. I ate an oyster for the first time, which I hated. I drank two more glasses of sauvignon blanc and laughed loudly at Eddie's jokes about chess, having been primed by memes for two months.

Dessert was a medley of three chocolate mousses — dark, chocolate, and white — arranged cleverly on a plate with many dottings and smears of sauces around and on top of them. As I ate it, I considered the evening. Facing the wall, I did not have much opportunity to consider the opinions of the other diners and what they might be thinking about my date with Eddie. The food tasted great, and I enjoyed eating it and could even eat all of it without getting too nervous. Eddie had been nice to me, and although I did not want to be his girlfriend, I had gotten a free dinner and I thought he had had a pretty fun time with me. I turned around to watch everyone eating, talking, and laughing together. They were not thinking about me.

As I watched, I felt a light pressure on my forearm. I turned. Eddie had placed his hand on my arm and was stroking it lightly with one of his fingers.

"So, Josie," he said, "want to head back to my place? There's this anime I think you'll really like."

I withdrew my arm involuntarily, shocked by what he said. This was not an outcome of the evening I had considered. "Oh!" I said.

"Oh, no. I couldn't. I have work in the morning, I need to sleep soon." I paused. "Besides, aren't you a little young for me?"

"I'm twenty-four!" he said, sounding indignant.

"Oh! Oh, yeah, that makes sense. Excuse me, gotta pee." I did a cartoonish running motion that I hoped would signal to Eddie that everything was A-OK.

In the bathroom I had diarrhea. In the mirror, I saw that I was drunk. My mascara was flaking onto my undereye bags.

When I returned to the table Eddie was swirling a tumbler of whisky around slowly. I ordered a tea and tried to smile a lot in case Eddie was upset that I wasn't going home with him.

"Well, thank you for a nice evening," I said to Eddie as he helped me pull on my coat, at his insistence. "I had a fun time, I enjoyed speaking with you."

"As did I, Miss Josie," he said, allowing a hand to linger a little longer on my shoulder. As we walked into the night, Millie and the other waiter stood smoking together, chatting and watching us shuffle off, too tired to make fun of us.

"So, you're sure I can't tempt you with another glass of wine at my place?" he said.

"Definitely not," I said. "I really, really have to go home. Thank you for inviting me, though. I hope you'll let me send you some money to pay you back for this evening, it was too much."

"Never," he said. He gazed at me for a long time. I wondered if he was going to wink, or lean in to kiss me. I averted my eyes. "Can I walk you home?"

"Of course." I wondered if he thought *I* would invite him in.

"Can I hold your hand?" he asked.

"Uhhhhhhhh," I said. "Not tonight."

"Not a problem." The walk was five minutes, and I talked the entire way, terrified Eddie would use any lulls to ask me more romantic questions.

At my door, I said thank you again. I was so worried he would kiss me that I could have vomited. He said goodbye and pulled me in for a hug, which lasted a very long time.

"Oh, Josie," he half-moaned. I stood still, and when he finally withdrew I was sure to turn my face away from his, which was turned toward mine, perhaps hoping to catch my mouth.

"Well, goodnight," I said, and went inside, shutting the door behind me firmly. Once alone in the entryway, I shuddered all over.

"Soooooooooooooo, how was it?" Logan asked, pointedly blinking her big doe eyes at me as I entered the living room.

"It was … it was many things," I said. I was already considering the evening, aware that this experience would probably be funny to tell other people about. I wished I wasn't such a terrible writer, otherwise I probably could have put the dinner to paper and written an entertaining story about it.

The next week, I saw Eddie and Helen at game night, kissing and playing Scrabble again.

"So, according to Ricky, they *did* break up two weeks ago, but I guess they're back together now," Logan whispered to me.

That night, I didn't notice any perceptible change in Eddie's mannerisms and behaviour toward me. He still grinned toothily and referred to me as "Miss Josie." It was as if we hadn't shared an evening at all, and I could wipe it from my memory and nothing in my life would be amiss. I did turn my head once to find Helen shooting daggers at me before wrapping her arms around her boyfriend. *Fair enough*, I thought.

"To think," said Logan, "you had the chance to find out what it would be like to have sex with *Eddie*. That could've been you." She gestured indiscreetly to Helen. "With Eddie," she repeated for emphasis.

• • •

Barb thought it was important for me to tell her all about the evening, and she swore it wasn't just because she thought it was funny. She took her notepad and pen and drew a line down the middle of the page, writing "liked" and "disliked" on either side of the line. She asked me to tell her all the things I thought were great about the evening and about Eddie, and the things I didn't like so much.

"Ummmm. He said I was good-looking a few times. That was nice," I said, regretting the words as they came out of my mouth. What kind of a vain person says stuff like that?

"Great, great," Barb said, writing this down with gusto. "What else did you like?"

"Um ..." I had to think about this for some time. "He seemed attracted to me."

"Okay, okay, good," she said. "Attracted ... to ... you," she muttered as she wrote on the notepad. "Anything else?"

"Um, maybe we can come back to that column?"

For the "disliked" column I told Barb I didn't like that Eddie had been pushy about me going home with him, and gave me a long and sensual hug, and talked about anime for a lot of the night, and was a centrist, and ordered a glass of milk and called it a virgin White Russian.

"Oh, and he wears fedoras," I said.

"Great. That's all great." When she was done writing, she turned the chart around to show me. "Now you have a wonderful new experience that has given you data about what you like and what you don't like. Next time you meet someone, you can use this experience to know better what you want." I understood the function of this chart, but reading the bullet points back I wasn't sure I could call it wonderful.

Barb was big on accumulating data to apply to your future experiences. Whenever I came to her with an annoying conflict I had had with Hannah, she'd always say something like "this is great practice for when you have a boyfriend."

I think Barb thought it would be really good for me to get a boyfriend, maybe because she thought I wanted a boyfriend. I did want a boyfriend, but I didn't want anyone to know that, including her. You weren't supposed to want a boyfriend if you didn't have one, you were just supposed to get one when you weren't thinking about it. To say you want a boyfriend is to transform yourself into an undesirable type of person, one who has a hard time getting a boyfriend.

But haven't you always had a hard time getting a boyfriend? a Barb in my head asked me in response to this idea. *In fact, you've never had one. Wouldn't being honest with yourself and others about your intentions and desires put you more, not less, in the path of getting what you want?*

But that's humiliating, I responded in my head.

Or ... brave? said imaginary Barb, smiling wisely at me from her imaginary armchair.

I think this session is over.

Chapter 9

LATER IN FEBRUARY, THE FIRE DEPARTMENT HAD ITS FIRST real fire since I'd joined up. Someone had dropped something flammable into the big Dumpster bin at the local dump just outside of town. We got the alert at work, so Hannah, Logan, and I all had to leave to get ready.

I had never had to contend with a physical Dumpster fire, but I thought that surely putting one out would teach me to deal better with the metaphorical Dumpster fires that sometimes arise in life, like bad dates with guys who drink milk.

"Are you nervous?" I asked Logan and Hannah.

"Pffft, no!" said Logan. She said she was just happy we got to leave work to do something else.

"You know, it's important to still do things even when you're nervous," said Hannah.

"I know that," I said.

Jeremy, Janine, Eddie, and Ivan were all at the fire hall, in various stages of undress, when we arrived. We put on our uniforms and drove two trucks to the dump after filling them with so much water I was surprised I couldn't hear it sloshing around as we drove.

The Dumpster in question sat squarely in the middle of the dump. There was a big circular ditch dug out around it to prevent bears from getting into it and eating things. This meant we couldn't get that close to the bin itself.

The walls of the bin itself were pretty high, so the only way we could get any water into it from across the ditch was to angle the hose nozzles upward and hope that gravity would direct the stream to the right place. Hannah and Jeremy manned the two hoses, and Logan and I stood between Hannah and the truck holding the halfway point of the hose to prevent any kinks from developing.

Because none of us could actually see the fire, we had to judge whether we had put it out based on the smoke billowing out of the top, shifting and waning depending on the wind. When the smoke disappeared, Jeremy and Hannah would signal for Eddie and Janine to turn off the hose, only for the smoke to start up again a few minutes later. We spent two hours doing this on and off before the trucks ran out of water. Janine and Hannah went back to the station for more.

"There has got to be a better way to do this," Logan whispered to me as we sat in a snowbank beside a pile of garbage. "This is ridiculous." She was genuinely angry about this. To me, this marked a significant difference in our characters. Logan was always taking stock of the world around her and saying with complete certainty what was wrong with it and how it should change.

"The graphic design in this menu is not good," she had said about the menu of Granville's Coffee in Quesnel. "It is absolutely not okay that this store doesn't sell plungers," she'd concluded of the Jack O' Clubs earlier that month when our toilet was clogged. "It's ridiculous!"

When I thought about it, I also thought what we were doing to put out the fire was ineffective and pointless. But it never would have occurred to me to express this to Hannah or Jeremy, who were, at least compared to me, the experts. Logan didn't think too much about who was expert and who was an amateur, and considered instead whose perspective seemed to be most logical, regardless of whether there was missing information.

In some ways, I wanted to be more like Logan, who was often right about things even when it frustrated me to admit it. But I found it exhausting to imagine what it must be like to find fault in so many things, and to have such a rigid perspective on good and bad. Weren't we all participating in a melting pot of decision making, actively creating a world made up of personal tastes and moral codes that we got to bump up against and experience every day? Personally, I considered this one of the most interesting things about being alive, and the idea of stifling this experience with a sense of absolute certainty depressed me.

Hannah and Janine returned with the trucks, and we began our routine again. Things went according to the plan, until something changed and Hannah somehow lost control of her hose. The hose flew around in her arms, sending her body in many directions, jerking her around. Like my car drifting on ice, this happened in slow motion, trapped within a moment that refused to end. Eventually, Eddie and Janine were able to turn off the water, and Hannah's body slammed onto the ground.

It was difficult to understand what had happened, although we had seen everything. Hannah was motionless for many seconds, and then she sat up abruptly, evidently unbalanced but also smiling and laughing. We all gathered around her. We determined that she'd hit her head very hard on the ground when she fell backward. There was no blood, but she held her hand to her scalp, as if afraid it would burst open.

Janine and Hannah left together with one of the trucks, and afterward they would go to the hospital.

"Do you think it was my fault?" I asked Logan as they pulled away. I had been holding the middle of the hose to prevent kinks, and wondered if I'd involuntarily jerked the hose, or if I could have stopped it before she fell.

"Oh my God, of course not!" said Logan. "This obviously happened because no one knows what they're doing, I hate to say." I wasn't sure if this was entirely true, but I nodded anyway, at least happy to hear Logan didn't blame me.

I wondered what would happen to Hannah at the hospital. It was always easy to assume things were going to turn out fine, but what if they didn't? People got injuries that ruined their lives all the time. I would have felt very guilty if she was really hurt because we got along so poorly.

At the dump, we continued to spray water on the Dumpster into the evening, until it began to snow heavily. The constant, heavy barrage of wet, fat snowflakes suffocated the smoking mass in the Dumpster, and suddenly there was no fire anymore, and we were free to leave.

Hannah returned home with a concussion diagnosis at 10:00 p.m.

"I feel a little weird, but the doctor says it's mild." She shrugged. She got to take the next week off from work and wasn't allowed to use the computer for long periods of time.

• • •

My time at Barkerville was coming to an end, and I didn't know what would happen to me. I peered into my future again and saw nothing laid out before me, just as I had before finishing my undergraduate and master's degrees. The idea of moving back to Niagara, or figuring out some other plan, seemed untenable, logistically complicated, and expensive. I had had this idea that being in the right place at the right time would present me with a plan for the rest of my life, either preordained or too perfect to ignore. I had thought that place might be Wells. And yet here I was, lost again.

"Well, do you even want to stay?" Barb had asked when I saw her last. "You seem ... not that happy with your life here."

"Well, I mean, yes. I guess I want to be happy here. I want someone to ask me to stay."

"Like who?"

I didn't answer. "Like, if Brandon or Janine were leaving, everyone would be devastated. When Logan leaves, I know she'll leave behind lots of friends and memories. I don't think I'll leave anything behind."

"Maybe you will," said Barb.

• • •

Nancy sat me down in front of her desk and asked me what my plans were beyond the internship. I told her I didn't know, and that I was stressed out about it. I hadn't done anything remarkable at all as a curatorial intern, except manage to fall asleep in the archive. I hadn't even learned how to write grants. I'd forgotten to ask.

"Why don't you apply to be an interpreter? Agatha Thompson wants to hire a new one for this season to work in the Wendle House and the Victorian Schoolhouse."

"An interpreter?" I said. "Me?" This idea had not occurred to me before. Interpreting, dressing up like a historic person, and strolling around with an old timey voice to talk to tourists, always struck me as a job that you had to decide you wanted to do early in life, like ballet dancing or pro tennis.

"Yeah, I bet you'd be good at it. You're so" — she gestured ambiguously — "bubbly and sweet."

"Do you really think I'd be good at it?" I asked.

"Sure, why not!" she said. "I did it once when I was a teenager. It's a piece of cake."

It was hard for me to imagine the work of an interpreter being a piece of cake. It was essentially acting in an eight-hour, scriptless play five days a week. On the other hand, it seemed like a job a really special person would do, a job for someone who wasn't afraid of stuff. The idea that I could do this, and become that person by association, was too irresistible to pass up. Nancy gave me Agatha's email.

I wrote and rewrote a long email to Agatha, explaining why I wanted the job and what I thought I could bring to the role. I told her all about my degrees and tried to think of some interesting points I could make about history.

"I think narratives about history are crucial for both highlighting the history of the marginalized and bringing history of all kinds to the attention of the public. I would be pleased to apply the extensive skills and knowledge I have obtained throughout my academic career to this role," I wrote. Everything I said was more or less true, but it sounded like bullshit. Would Agatha actually buy this?

Agatha didn't even ask to interview me. She sent me an email with one line that read, "Would you like to be an interpreter this summer?" which struck me as a dramatic way to email someone you've never met.

Nonetheless, I laughed out loud when I read it. I was so relieved to have figured out my life for six more months. I marched around town with purpose and told everyone who would listen about my new job. Interpreters were the lifeblood of Barkerville, the public face. Didn't that make me an integral part of the community?

"We'll be co-workers, Henrick!" I said to him boldly at the bar. He smiled politely. Logan, on the other hand, was ecstatic, and did a little victory dance when I shared the news with her.

"Oooh oooh!" she said, gyrating her hips.

The comfort I experienced at finding a new situation was only replaced by dread when Agatha emailed me the script and preparation materials for interpretation, and I had to contemplate actually doing the job.

She asked me to meet her at her house so she could take measurements for my costumes. She lived down by the creek in a mobile home. It was poorly maintained, with higher snowbanks than I'd seen anywhere in town. Her house was the only structure on a long winding path. Brandon told me he'd heard crazy things about the house, but wouldn't say precisely what the rumors were.

Agatha was known to be reclusive, and was one of those people who stocked up on supplies all summer to avoid going into Quesnel during the winter. At the front door, I was greeted by a remarkably little woman, with a mess of greyed hair, halfway to white, piled on top of her head, and the gnarliest eyebrows I had ever seen on a woman, with long, rogue hairs going in all directions.

She beckoned me in with a solemnity I could tell was put on, or rehearsed, as if she was playing it for laughs.

The inside of her home was a sight to behold. She was probably a hoarder; her living space was packed to the brim with items, with a decently sized space for us to sit in the middle. It was, however, quite an organized mess: the magazines were stacked with the magazines, the clothing with the clothing, the cans with the cans.

Agatha sat me down on her little wicker sofa and somehow produced a cup of tea from her kitchen, which was packed to the brim with non-perishables that made a sort of fortress around her appliances.

"Interpretation," Agatha began, as I sipped from a chipped porcelain teacup, "is not acting. I am not an actor. *Some* people think of this job as an opportunity to practice their acting skills, to entertain guests with humour and improv. I do not think of it this way." I could tell Agatha had given this speech many times before.

"I" — she paused again for dramatic effect — "am a storyteller, *not* an actor. *You*" — she paused again, employing suspense particularly well for someone insisting they are not an actor — "will also be a storyteller. I do not expect you to dance like a monkey for tourists. We are there to teach visitors about history through stories. A well-told story can be the most effective thing in the world, and those stories will be what keep visitors coming back year after year."

"I agree with you," I said. I told her about my relationship to history and how I truly felt it had been facilitated through stories, which led the way to more focused and academic study.

"Precisely!" she responded.

I liked Agatha, I decided. I asked her why we hadn't met before.

"Oh, I don't get out much," she said, beginning another speech. "I find I don't crave company like I used to. No, I have everything I need right here." She gestured around at all of her possessions. To be fair, she did have a lot of stuff to keep her entertained.

She told me she used to be a social worker, and had three grown-up sons and had been married once in Ontario, but they'd divorced long ago. Then she had moved to Ireland for two years, and had a relationship there.

"It ended poorly," she said, her hand to the side of her mouth like an actor giving an aside. People and wall decals were always saying "life is short," but observing Agatha it occurred to me that life was very long, with space for many lives. This idea was both thrilling and slightly sickening.

Agatha brought out a mess of corsets, fabrics, and premade costumes for us to sift through. She handed me a pink corset and helped me to pull it tightly around my torso. The pressure on my ribcage and stomach was terrible.

"By the end of the summer, this will probably be too big for you," she said. "Corsets rearrange your body and move your organs around to make your waist smaller."

"Hmmm," I said, feeling guilty about moving my organs around to give myself a smaller waist. I thought I should be anti–waist training, even if it's work mandated.

"No matter what you hear, corsets are not any of that anti-feminism anti-woman nonsense," said Agatha, as if reading my thoughts. "Corsets were actually designed to make housework easier for a woman. They didn't manipulate her shape by design, it's simply a side effect, albeit an attractive one." By having me lift her ottoman, she showed me how, when in the corset, I was forced to lift with my knees and not my back. "See?" she said. "Women could lift almost six times what they can today with no corset. When the corset went out of fashion things changed much for the working woman, who no longer had the benefit of all of that support."

In Agatha's mirror I admired my waist, newly tiny, as conspicuously as I could. The garment had pushed all of the fat from my belly area downward, giving me the appearance of having a large, spacious womb, like women in renaissance paintings. My breasts were similarly pushed upward so they sat higher and were more buoyant on top. It felt almost too convenient that I could make my body look like this and simply argue that it was actually better for me, and actually feminist, because I could lift heavier stuff.

Agatha and I would be sharing responsibilities for the Wendle House, a typical Barkerville home, and the schoolhouse, where guests could come and pretend to be Victorian students. Confusingly, the Wendle House was "set" in the Edwardian era around 1910, while the schoolhouse was meant to reflect the 1870s, around the time of the true gold rush. As interpreters, we'd need to switch between the periods depending on where we were assigned that day.

"People didn't just leave when the gold rush was over, you know," Agatha said. "People stuck around until it became a park in the 1950s! That's the point of the Wendle House."

Two time periods meant two sets of outfits.

For the Wendle House, Agatha dressed me up like Mary Poppins, handing me a bunch of puffy shirts and long skirts, and plopping a straw hat on my head and fitting it with a pin. I liked the way it looked so much that I felt like a pervert.

For the Victorian era, Agatha dressed me in a big purple getup with a high neckline and an enormous skirt and a bonnet that I thought was hideous on me.

Agatha advised me to practise my scripts, but didn't seem to too worried about my sticking to what was written. "Develop your own style!" she said enthusiastically.

• • •

For administrative reasons that were not altogether clear to me, I'd have to move out of the staff house when my internship was over, and I wouldn't be allowed to live there in the summer. Instead, Sharon presented me a photo of a new staff compound the park was building. At first glance, it resembled a bunch of old storage units pushed together.

"It's made of old storage units we pushed together. It's very functional."

"Huh," I said. *Life is very long*, I thought to myself.

Sharon also offered me the position of "camp caretaker" in exchange for free rent.

"It'll be some sort of cross between a residence advisor and a janitor," she said. "A lot of the people living in the camps will be right out of high school, some of them away for the first time. We're hiring two people, so you wouldn't have to do it alone." I pictured myself, interpreter by day and hard-working, beloved caretaker by night. The fact that Sharon had even offered me the role, without my having to ask, must have meant that she had a good opinion of me. This was thrilling, because Sharon was hard to read, with her impassive face, and so I could only rely on her words.

Logan was beside herself when I told her I was moving out. "You can't leave me alone with *her*!" She was practically shouting. We were in my car, on the way to Quesnel for groceries.

"She likes you way better than me, you'll be fine," I told her.

"Are you kidding? Compared to me, she's basically obsessed with you."

"Seriously? She loves you! She hates me!" We spent the car ride discussing which one of us Hannah disliked more. We determined that Logan probably annoyed her more with her directness, but that she was more competitive with me because we worked in the same department, which, for Hannah, was maybe a more powerful feeling than annoyance.

Chapter 10

MY WORK IN THE ARCHIVE ENDED WITHOUT CEREMONY. I wasn't leaving, so no one actually needed to say goodbye. I went back to Ontario for a month and practised the scripts over and over in my parents' car so no one would hear me, wondering when my own unique and personal script would emerge from the pre-written one, as Agatha had wanted. I tried to improvise but it sounded so stupid every time.

At night, I had bad dreams about my ugly Victorian dress falling to pieces in front of my class, which was made up of members of the Canadian House of Commons, or inside of a sinkhole. I woke up agitated, and considered emailing Agatha to tell her she needed to find someone else while there was still time.

When I arrived back in the Cariboo, it was late April. The trip back now felt familiar and mundane in a comforting way that made me proud, as if knowing it made it mine.

While Ontario had burst into spring while I was home, northern B.C. had not changed much, season-wise. The air was certainly much warmer, and the roads cleared of any ice or snow, but the snowbanks were still substantial, and at the gas stations and rest stops everyone still wore their warmest jackets.

At the staff house, which was no longer my house, Logan wrapped me in a big bear hug before ushering me into the living room and catching me up on all the latest gossip around town. Brandon had a new girlfriend, an artist named Ailish who made experimental soundscapes.

"How alluring," I said.

Jeremy was seeing someone new, too. Another interpreter. "It's quite the scandal. She's *twenty-two*," said Logan.

"Oh, woah. How old is Jeremy anyway? Thirty-four?"

"He's *thirty-nine*," Logan said.

"Oh," I said.

"Janine and Hannah are pissed. It's caused quite the stir." Logan said this with some glee. I knew Logan looked down on people who clutched pearls too much, and when they did it made her feel superior, even if the matter at hand was worth clutching pearls over. In any case, it was hard for me to be shocked by this news because it sounded fake, like something that only happened in movies where adult women get left by their shitty professor husbands for grad students.

Suddenly, a person I had never seen appeared in the doorway of the living room. He was Mike, the summer curatorial intern, fresh out of his second year of university.

"*Heyyyy*, Mikey Mike," said Logan warmly. "Are we still watching *The Avengers* later?" I flushed hot with jealousy as she spoke. It hadn't occurred to me that there would be someone in my place when I got back. It was times like this that made me so aware that I had no control over anything. If I got married, I wouldn't be able to prevent my husband from leaving me for a grad student, just like I couldn't prevent Logan from getting bored of me.

Mike had slicked-back black hair like Jimmy Stewart, and he wore a sensible knit sweater. He looked a schoolboy from the nineteenth century. He greeted us shyly.

"He's kind of weird," Logan whispered, her voice changing completely, when he left to go to the basement. "He plays vintage video games down there all day. He brought all these old consoles." She chuckled. "Hannah loves him." I sighed, relieved.

Logan wanted to go to the pub because they'd just gotten a new type of IPA there, but I had to go to meet Sharon at the staff compound, my new home. It was in the woods, on a dirt path smack dab between Wells and Barkerville. Sharon was waiting for me outside when I arrived. Gazing up at the ugly building, I was reminded of a clunky spaceship or a 3D model of a nuclear bomb shelter.

Sharon took me inside and introduced me to Dougie, who was the other caretaker. Dougie was in his fifties and had a big black moustache. He wore brown overalls. We were the first two residents at the camp.

"Yello," he said, and shook my hand heftily. Sharon took us around the site and showed us all the features of the rooms. There were blackout curtains on each window, and the kitchen was outfitted with four stations, each with its own appliances and pots and pans.

We sat in wobbly chairs at a wobbly table in the kitchen and discussed the new job. Dougie said, in no uncertain terms, that he did not want to have to interact with the residents if it could be avoided.

"Listen, I'm a bachelor," he said, wringing his enormous hands. "I can't say I know too much about talking to kids or anything. I can do anything to do with cleaning or whatever but I think you should be the one to talk to everyone about rules and stuff."

I couldn't believe my luck. I hated cleaning, and was generally a slob. "Mmmm, you know, that could work," I said, nodding my head in a way I hoped appeared pensive, not wanting Dougie to realize the amazing deal I was getting. We agreed to split the role, and I would be the one to do all the social stuff. Dougie looked relieved.

When the meeting was done, I lay in my new twin bed. It was uncomfortable. The walls were made of metal. My room was tiny, and I became aware that my quality of life had decreased without access to my big bed at the staff house and a living room with a TV and couches. That night, I returned to Wells and went to the pub with Logan, before falling asleep on the living room couch. In the morning, I opened my eyes to see Hannah, peering down at me. I jumped.

"Oh, Hannah, you surprised me!"

"Okay?" she said.

• • •

Leading up to Barkerville's opening weekend, Wells and the compound began to fill up with seasonal workers. A fish and chips shop, a taco joint, and other exciting businesses cropped up in food trucks and buildings that had been empty all winter. Logan and I visited them after she was done work each day, eager to explore the sudden diversity in the local cuisine. A jump from two restaurants to five is a 150 percent increase, after all.

The residents at the compound were, for the most part, very young. Their intake documents revealed that most of them were seventeen or eighteen, just on summer break from school or off to college the next year. One boy, John, was eighteen but could have passed for thirteen, and wore a big cowboy hat that could have swallowed him up if it folded in on itself. Sharon told me, privately, that his dad was a big oil guy in Alberta. Many of them worked for the various businesses in Barkerville. One boy, Jason, was an intern for Island Mountain arts, and Min, the girl I recognized from Chinatown when I first arrived in Barkerville in the fall, was an interpreter like me.

In the first few days after arrival, John quickly formed a clique with a girl named Riley, who had green hair that she was considering turning into dreadlocks, and Roger, a very tall, lanky teenager with watery eyes who appeared uncomfortable in his skin. The three of them made themselves at home in the kitchen each day and had a habit of playing Dungeons & Dragons deep into the night.

I appreciated them because their charisma was so flimsy and easily revealed their awkward age, and yet all of their peers were deeply impacted by their presence in one way or another. There were twenty-seven residents in total, and most of them either wanted to be friends with them, shyly offering them compliments, or found them explosively irritating and rolled their eyes as they made up goofy songs on the ukulele at dinner time.

My favourite resident was Bobby. She was a curatorial assistant with long shiny hair and a round face. As I handed her the keys when I checked her in, she accepted them with a small smirk, as if remembering a private joke about room keys. She was twenty-one, had just graduated from her degree in archaeology at Simon Fraser University. She told me she wanted to begin her master's degree in a year or so.

"I studied archaeology for my master's," I told her. It was the first time in forever that someone had aspired to do something I had already done.

"Oh, wow, really?" she said. She told me she was interested in geospatial imaging. "What did you specialize in?"

"Um, mostly buildings, medieval stuff," I said, not wanting to say "movies!"

"That is so cool," said Bobby.

"Yeah, it was pretty cool," I said. Feeling brave and powerful, I asked her if she wanted to go to the pub later.

"Oh, without a doubt," she said, as if we were already friends.

Bobby showed me her big blue pickup truck that she'd bought for $2,000 before leaving Vancouver for Wells. A canoe was haphazardly tied to the top. "It cost me almost all my savings, but it gets the job done," she said, smacking the side.

"How adventurous," I said. It sounded sarcastic, but I meant it. I wanted Bobby to like me, so I insisted we drive in my car.

Daniel, the youthful interpreter who would portray Barkerville's priest in the summer, asked if he could come with us. I couldn't tell by his question if he was meeting someone there, or if he was also asking if he could hang out with us. I felt too awkward to ask, so I didn't say anything.

Halfway there, it occurred to me that as the camp caretaker I should only be driving people to a bar if they're of age, and that Daniel's appearance gave me few clues about whether he was over nineteen. He had good skin, but no facial hair. A weak chin, but bags under his eyes.

"So ... how old are you, Daniel?" I asked him, trying to sound casual about it. Daniel had one of those demeanours where, when you turned to address him, he already had a well-practised and uneasy smile on his face, as if trying to anticipate what you would do or say and offer you his approval right away to avoid upsetting you. This type of boy always made me anxious, and sometimes angry. After all, I wasn't scary, or at risk of getting upset, was I? Why did people like that want to please others so much, like their lives depended on it?

Sounds a bit like you, I imagined Barb saying if I were to tell her about this.

"I'm twenty-four," said Daniel.

"Oh, okay then," I said, smiling at him in the rearview mirror. "What year were you born? I turned twenty-five in January."

"Ninety-four."

"Oh, same age."

"Yup, same age." Another nervous grin.

"What do you do during the rest of the year?" I asked. Our conversation was clunky, and I turned to Bobby, hoping she could enliven it, but she was quiet, preoccupied with the scenery.

"I'm a student."

"Oh? And … what do you study?"

"Well, I'm in seminary school."

"Seminary school?"

"Like, to be a priest?" He delicately elaborated, sounding apologetic that he hadn't explained it better the first time.

"Oh, wow!" I said, with genuine surprise. I regretted this exclamation, because I was sure that people were always reacting to this information this way. I tried to think of what an intelligent and not-nosy person would ask about this. "What, uh, you know, kind? Denomination, I mean."

"Um, Anglican?" he said.

"When I was little my family and I went to a United Church. We, uh, really liked our minister."

"Hmmm, that makes sense. You remind me of a few of my United Church friends."

"I do?" I tried to imagine what exactly made someone United Church-y.

"Yeah, similar energies."

"Huh. Well, I don't go anymore," I said, suddenly worried that he might try to encourage me to become Anglican. I tried to change the topic. "Where do you study?"

"McGill. In Montreal?"

"I did my undergrad there!"

"Me, too," said Daniel, smiling at me priestfully. This information excited me more than I realized it would. I wanted to slam my hand down on the horn in celebration.

"You did? Did you graduate in 2016?"

"That I did." His face was boyish and he had unfortunate sideburns that extended just a little bit too long underneath his floppy brown hair. I tried to imagine him in the context of McGill, surrounded by rich kids and buying samosas in the Leacock building between classes. He didn't remind me of anyone I knew there.

"I wonder if we know any of the same people," he said.

I thought about this, but I didn't mention any names. Thinking of my time at McGill sometimes nauseated me.

"What did you study?" I asked.

"Well, religion," he said, smiling kindly if a bit sardonically.

"Oh, yeah," I said. "Duh!" We both laughed, like real friends.

Just a few minutes earlier, I'd been annoyed by Daniel because of his hyperreactive face. Now I thought he was cool and wanted to be his best friend. How could I be trusted to make judgments about anything or anyone?

At the pub, we all convened at a table with Logan, who was sitting with Mike, Janine, Henrick, and the other Richfield judges, who had just returned to Wells only a few days earlier. Over the winter they had all lived together in an apartment in Vancouver. There were three of them, but there had only been one bedroom.

"To save money," Greg Chapman explained.

Daniel agreed to drive us back to the compound, so I was free to drink as much as I wanted, and I downed three pints faster than I meant to. Talking to a bunch of young people in a group was exhilarating, like being part of a celebrity's entourage or on the cheerleading squad. There was a sense of power that I knew could vanish at any second if I said the wrong thing or acted like a loser. Logan told everyone she thought my car playlists were weird, and I knew it was imperative that I keep my cool. I shrugged coolly and held my breath until I was sure the conversation had shifted to a new topic.

On the other end of the table across from Bobby, Logan, Daniel, Janine, and I, the judges were goofing off, doing mysterious physical comedy and loudly reciting what must have been ancient inside jokes, forged in their many summers together as interpreters. Greg was folding napkins into little hats and trying to forcefully put them on Josh's head. I somehow wished they would include me. Why were men so much more intriguing than women, even when they were acting like dumbasses? I noticed even Bobby's and Logan's eyes drifted toward them throughout the night as well.

"So, Janine, is Wells crazy in the summer?" asked Bobby at one point.

"It can get pretty wild," she said, nodding her head and smiling mischievously, as if she were remembering things that she wasn't going to share with us.

"What is there, like, insane drama? Or, like, forbidden Barkerville romances?" Bobby asked.

Janine's face dropped. "Well, I wouldn't know anything about that. I don't think it's nice to gossip about people." She crossed her arms.

Bobby was stricken. "Oh, no, neither do I!" she sputtered. I could have laughed, if I didn't feel so terrible for her.

"Is your name short for Roberta?" I asked her in an effort to divert the conversation away.

"It's just Bobby."

"My name isn't short for Josephine, either," I said. "When I was twelve my parents asked me if I wanted to change it to Josephine, but by that time it was too late. It would have been crazy to make the switch to Josephine after twelve years of being just Josie."

"My parents named me after Bobby Orr," she said, sounding embarrassed. My dad loved Bobby Orr.

"Do you like hockey?"

"Not really."

At the end of the evening, I passed Daniel my keys and he drove Bobby and I back to the compound.

"That was soooo fun," I said, leaning my head against the side door window.

• • •

The next morning, I drove myself and Daniel to Barkerville for the first day of interpreter orientation.

"Do you think you'll be a good interpreter?" I asked Daniel. The bags under his eyes were even bigger than the day before.

"I don't know. I'm pretty shy."

"Yeah, I dunno about me either. Who knows, maybe we'll be great."

"Maybe we will," Daniel replied. Neither of us sounded convincing.

The first day of orientation began with an enormous breakfast buffet at the Wake-Up Jake, one of the two operational restaurants in the park. Inside it was styled like a Victorian fine dining establishment, and served typical twenty-first century brunch fare out of buffet trays.

I was overwhelmed with nerves and only took a modest helping of breakfast foods, and then I was too shy to get up in front of everyone for seconds. I watched Greg Chapman fill his plate with breakfast meats and then go back for seconds, then thirds. I was charmed watching him pack away bacon strip after bacon strip into his cylindrical frame, looking slightly self-conscious but also like he was enjoying his breakfast immensely.

Across the room, I could see Jeremy sitting next to a skinny girl. She was young, like a teenager. He whispered something in her ear, and she laughed.

Sheena, who had also returned to interpret for the summer, followed my gaze and noticed Jeremy and his girlfriend. "I'm disgusted," she said irritably. "He and I are basically the same age. The men in this town are ridiculous."

Across the table, Daniel, who may or may not have had any idea what Sheena was talking about, nodded sympathetically.

"Don't try to find a man here, Josie," she said, shaking her head vigorously. "They'll just leave you when you get wrinkly and saggy like us old ladies." This comment annoyed me, because it seemed like it was about me and my situation as a young woman, but it was actually about Sheena's perspective on her own life.

I turned to Daniel, to see how he was taking this. I was amused to see that his face was overcome with an extremely guilty expression, like if he wasn't careful, he'd transform into one of these wife-leaving men.

I looked back at Jeremy and the skinny girl. I couldn't tell if I was supposed to feel cheated on behalf of the more age-appropriate women in town, or on behalf of myself, or like Jeremy was disgusting, and taking advantage of her. I didn't know what it was like to have a boyfriend, so I didn't know what it would feel like to be twenty-two and have an old boyfriend. In spite of myself, I was impressed and jealous that she had been able to make a guy like her on purpose.

I had never seriously thought about my age positively or negatively impacting my sexual viability. I had only ever kissed or been on dates with guys who were basically the same age as me. It hadn't occurred to me that I could date someone as old as Jeremy, or that he would ever have wanted to.

"Are you even allowed to date?" Sheena asked Daniel, still sounding grumpy. "As a Catholic priest?"

"Well, I'm Anglican. And I'm married. So yes, but also no." He held up his left hand and wiggled his fingers, revealing a gold band I hadn't noticed before.

"You're married?" I blurted out.

"For three years now." He explained that his wife was named Louisa, and she was a professional cellist who taught music to children on the side. Daniel was quickly becoming the most surprising person I had met in a long time.

I was so impressed by people who didn't give every interesting thing about themselves away as soon as they met someone new. I sometimes tried being like this, but always failed spectacularly. Remembering the night before, I'd already shared with Daniel where I was from, what my parents did, what I studied in school, and what I'd had for dinner the day before.

Charles, in his capacity as development officer, and Sharon made a rousing speech welcoming the interpretive staff to the 2019 season, declaring that it would be the most successful and exciting year to date. The interpreters whooped and cheered. The judges spun their napkins above their heads, which made everyone laugh.

After breakfast, I met Agatha at the Wendle House. The house itself was two-storied and covered in white clapboard. It reminded me of a Grandma Moses painting. Inside, Agatha quizzed me on the plethora of antique (or else antique-looking) kitchen and cookware items. She gave a detailed explanation of each item, her eyes twinkling as she described her crinkle-cut vegetable slicer. I tried to match her enthusiasm, although my energy had waned slightly by the time she got around to explaining the ice box, my last piece of Edwardian kitchen equipment.

"Now, where do you keep the ice?" she asked me, gesturing to the little brown cube. It had two little doors, one on top of the other.

"Ummm, this one?" I said, pointing to the bottom one. She shook her head and smirked wryly.

"Wrong." She opened the top door. "The ice goes on this little platform here. Because cool air" — she paused, pointing downward — "sinks. And hot air" — she paused again, moving her hands upward — "rises."

"Oh, wow," I said, aware that I'd already said "oh, wow" to her upward of one hundred times that morning.

After the lesson, all of the interpreters gathered outside of St. Saviour's Church, where Daniel would be working. There, Ivan, the sexy blacksmith, gave a rigorous tutorial on the topic of chopping firewood.

"You don't have to worry about this part," whispered Agatha to me, "Ivan chops all of our wood in exchange for free cake."

Back at the compound, I found John and his friends playing Cards Against Humanity in the kitchen. Behind them, there were small piles of dishes in each sink. I stared at the plates and bowls for a moment or two, trying to decide what to do.

Before anyone had moved in, enforcing the no-dirty-dishes policy in the kitchen had been an entirely conceptual idea that had seemed like an easy task. I realized then that I hadn't actually come up with a strategy for enforcing it beyond telling people about the rule.

"Hmmm, did some people leave their dishes to soak today?" I said, looking directly at no one as if I was talking to myself.

"Ummm, maybe?" said Riley, who wore a dangly earring in one ear. They were all now shrugging back toward their game.

"Oh, okay then!" I said. The smile on my face felt physically too big for the situation, but it was fine because they weren't watching me anyway. "I know we all know, but don't forget to make sure we clean our dishes … as soon as we use them!" I couldn't stop using the plural second person. The teens nodded, but didn't say anything. "Okay then!" I said again, and I left the kitchen feeling fully aware of my body, like when you walk by a man who is obviously checking out your ass.

I knocked on Bobby's door. She called for me to come in. I found her on her bed, outfitted with a comforter featuring a mandala pattern, reading *This Changes Everything* by Naomi Klein.

"Wassup?" she said, snapping the book shut and smiling sleepily at me.

"What are you up to?"

"Not much. Wanna go to Bowron Lake? We could have a beer."

"That would be great." I was overjoyed that she had suggested hanging out before I had to. We wore the warmest coats we had, and stopped at the Jack first to buy tall individual cans of stout and blonde ales.

The drive to Bowron Lake was about thirty minutes, following a wide gravel road that twisted and turned manically. I had done this drive infrequently enough to be cognizant of its beauty, silently marvelling at the way the way the trees stood against the sky and the surprise of the unexpected dips along the path. Bobby's truck engine made a loud rumbling sound, and it compounded with the sound of the crunching dirt and gravel on the crude road into the national park so that we could barely hear her Lana Del Rey album playing.

"I love Lana," I said.

"Me, too, she's the best." She let me flip through the catalogue of CDs in her truck.

"There's no aux jack. Too old," Bobby explained.

I pawed through Bon Iver, Lana, Fleetwood Mac, Big Thief, The Cranberries, Sky Ferreira.

"Oh my God!" I said, holding up the *Twilight* soundtrack.

"It's so fire," she said. She took the CD from me, ejected the Lana disk, and replaced it in the reader. She turned the volume up as "Supermassive Black Hole" began to play. I had gotten so used to spending time with Logan and Hannah, two people with whom I shared few material interests. Already, things flowed so easily between me and Bobby that I almost felt guilty about it, like I was betraying Logan by having more fun with someone else. Who was she going to hang out with when I was with Bobby?

We reached Bowron Lake. There was a small motel resort, empty of guests, just farther down the shoreline with various cottages and rental businesses along the road that led deeper into the park. We stopped right at the water's edge. Across the lake were two large peaks, and between them the Rocky Mountains poked through.

We took our beers and sat on the steps of a deserted hut advertising canoe rentals. We clinked our cans and sipped, first sitting quietly and taking in the calm water, which was protected from any wind by the mountains. The water was clear and it was easy to see to the floor where we sat, revealing small fish. We took in the view for a few minutes, before we began viciously gossiping.

I told her about Hannah, and about how Janine loves to do impressions of gay men and make other people feel guilty.

"Oh my God, she was so stressful!" said Bobby. "What a bitch!" I had not called Janine a bitch before, although I might have if I was given the opportunity. Nevertheless, hearing the words gave me a jolt.

"Yeah, she is," I said. I couldn't stop telling her things, my opinions about everyone and everything in Wells. I told her about Logan's friend Ruben, and about Eddie and the virgin White Russian. My mouth opened and closed at lightning speed, only slowing down for a minute every so often to survey Bobby's face to see if she was getting annoyed at me. She wasn't. On the contrary, she watched me intently, hungry for more information. She laughed at all my jokes.

We talked about how neither of us had ever had boyfriends.

"It's not a big deal," I said, my eyes darting over to her. "I mean, who cares?"

"Yeah, it's cool!" said Bobby.

"I'm so happy that you're here," I said, and I really meant it. I thought we were like two characters at the beginning of an exciting, coming-of-age novel. We stayed out until eleven, when the sky was just turning to night. I was exhilarated by my time with Bobby. She was so young, even younger than me, and full of life, with opinions just like mine. I considered the months to come with breathless anticipation. Something exciting, no, transformative, was bound to happen, wasn't it?

• • •

For the next two weeks, the Barkerville staff and interpreters continued to prepare for opening weekend in the middle of the month. The curatorial staff repaired broken signs and swept the ground of debris and dead leaves left by the quickly melting snow. The stablemaster arrived with seven horses to operate the stagecoach. As the temperatures warmed incrementally by the day, groundhogs appeared at Barkerville and in Wells en masse.

"Whistle pigs," Brandon said to me, angling his iPhone at one of them, trying to get a photo for the Barkerville Instagram page. "Sure, they're cute, but they're also fucking annoying."

Logan had been correct, Brandon had a new girlfriend, named Ailish. She had come as a visiting artist while I was home in Niagara. While she was visiting, they had fallen in love and were now a bona fide couple. I met her at the pub for game night one evening. She had long, thick black hair and a freckly nose. I wondered if he had told her that his type was girls with long, thick black hair and freckly noses.

Ailish was good-looking, much better looking than I was, and I tried to figure out why she wanted to become Brandon's girlfriend while I didn't. I thought people who were more beautiful were, as a rule, pickier than people who were less beautiful, and this outcome seemed to be a glitch in the system.

"Maybe beauty is subjective," suggested Barb when I posited this dilemma to her.

"If you say so, Barb," I replied.

During the workday, I practised my scripts for Agatha. This was mortifying.

"At this point, you need to make sure the audience is drawn into the lesson, or else it will be pandemonium," she said during a lull in my presentation of the "spelling bee" portion of the script. The discomfort of performing compounded with the even more excruciating ordeal of being critiqued made me defensive and grouchy when she offered feedback. I knew this wasn't fair, and I said thank you each time, trying not to appear emotional.

Agatha had me wear my corset while I practised so that I would get used to the sensation of wearing one all day and wouldn't be uncomfortable or physically stilted come opening weekend. It gave me a terrible backache and made slouching impossible, and if I was sitting I had to grab on to something when I stood again, or else I'd fall backward.

"You'll get used to it eventually," she said cheerfully as I hauled myself out of one of the desks in the schoolhouse.

In the evenings, I hung out with Bobby. We went to the pub, or to Bowron, or drank beers at the fire pit by the compound in the evenings, inviting each other everywhere we went, just like I had done with Logan months before.

"Is that your sister?" Ricky asked me, seeing us together at the pub for a second night in a row. "Did she move here from Ontario as well? You're so alike." I beamed, and explained that no, we were just new friends. Bobby and I smiled at one another.

I told Bobby what training was like, and she complained about Mike. "He's so weird. I think he's a conservative," she said, in falsely hushed tones. "And he can't cook. Did you know he brought like forty cans of baked beans to Wells with him? Isn't that weird?"

"That is pretty weird," I said. Bobby and Mike worked together in the curatorial department. They were supervised by a senior curatorial assistant named Marcia, who was fifty and went everywhere with her massive boxer mix. During the day, the three of them spent all their time together. Some nights, Bobby and Mike went to Marcia's RV in Wells and smoked weed together. She would come back and tell me all the strange or annoying things Mike had said and done.

"I tried to mess up his hair, right? Like, as a joke, obviously," she explained. "Get this: he got so pissed. But, like, actually pissed. He got really quiet, and, like, wouldn't talk to me for, like, fifteen minutes." I didn't know Mike that well, but the way Bobby described him made me laugh really hard.

Between work and nights with Bobby, I didn't see Logan until a week later, on our regularly scheduled visit to Quesnel together. It was awkward to try to switch back into "Logan mode," to laugh at her jokes and put my own opinions aside in an effort understand hers better, like trying to fit a slept-on mattress back into its airtight packaging.

"What song is this?" Logan asked when a song she didn't recognize came on, letting out her classic, exasperated laugh as she did. I shuffled the playlist and scowled.

• • •

The night before opening weekend, the judges hosted a bonfire at their cottage in Wells. I was jealous that they got to live in a house. Their lucky living situation seemed somehow connected to or even because everyone found them funny and thought they were cool. Bobby and I drove a bunch of people from the staff compound, and we all sat around the fire roasting hot dogs. Jeremy and his girlfriend, whose name I learned was Martine, were there, making out on a tree trunk fashioned into a bench. "That's fucked up," Bobby whispered to me.

I sat on one side of Bobby and Mike, who ended up in a loud argument about whether Harry Potter should be read as a gay character or an allegory for gayness. Listening to them, it was very clear that Mike didn't understand the nature of the argument.

"But he likes Cho Chang, Bobby, remember? And Ginny! He's not gay!" he said, exasperated.

"Yeah, but he represents being gay! C'mon, Harry comes out of a *closet*? And it doesn't actually matter what J.K. Rowling *wrote*, it's about reading between the lines. It's clear that everyone is gay. Except Ron, obviously."

"That makes no sense," he said. Bobby stuck her tongue out at him, and he began tickling her. She screamed and wriggled around in his arms.

I was not interested in trying to participate in whatever was happening beside me. To my right, Greg Chapman, the bacon-enjoying judge, sat roasting a hot dog quietly.

"Um, are you having a, a nice summer so far?" I asked him. Greg was definitely the strangest judge, with his stringy hair and awkward posture. In the skits I had seen at the cabaret in October before he had left town, he had usually played the weird guy, and easily slipped into being the butt of the joke. This made me like him most out of all of the judges.

"Yeah, definitely," he said, taking a sip of Cariboo beer. I asked him if he liked being a judge, and he said he did, because he got to do improv every day and hang out with his best friends. He said best friends somewhat forcefully, like it was a point of pride for him, or like I might not think he was really part of their gang. He was twenty-five, like me, and he told me he was waiting to hear back from the Iowa Writer's Workshop.

"Oh, wow," I said. I knew that was an impressive program because that's where Lena Dunham's character had gone on HBO's *Girls*. Greg must have been a wonderful writer to think he was talented enough to apply there.

"I'm a writer, too," I said, mostly lying. He told me his biggest influences were David Foster Wallace and Philip Roth. I said mine was Daphne du Maurier, even though nothing I had ever written sounded like her at all.

"What do you like about Daphne du Maurier?" he asked.

"She's ..." I began, searching for the right word, "evil."

Greg and I had a lot in common, as it turned out. We both loved the work of the comedian Matt Berry, but thought it was shitty how the creator of *The IT Crowd* was transphobic. Greg said that there should be more space for women in comedy, and in the Canadian writing community.

We were interrupted by John, who approached me. "Um, something's wrong with Roger?" he said. There was a giddy quality to his voice as he spoke, which confused me. He led me across the backyard to where Riley was sitting with Roger. He was wan.

"Roger has appendicitis!" Riley exclaimed. She and John were buzzing with manic energy, evidently stimulated by Roger's sudden health emergency.

"Shut up, Riley," said Roger, throwing a dirty paper plate at her.

She shrieked. "Abuser! You should be at the hospital, young man!" She threw the plate back at him.

I screwed up my face, trying to tune out Riley's voice and think of what to do next.

"Are you sure you have appendicitis?" I asked. He nodded. He told me the pain had started yesterday, but had only just gotten worse.

"Okay, okay. So, let's get you to the hospital," I said. With no cell reception, and my phone back at the compound, I drove Roger in my car to Barkerville where, we could call an ambulance on the security landline. Roger was too tall, and had to push the passenger seat way back to get his legs in.

At the park, I knocked on the security office door. We were greeted by a sleepy guard whose name tag read "Lance."

"Um, hi, Lance," I said. "We need to call an ambulance? Can we, uh, do that?" I realized I had not practised what I would say at all. Lance stared at me.

I tried again. "Okay, so Roger, one of the residents at the staff camp down the road, has appendicitis. Can you help us call an ambulance?"

"Oh, sure, sure," said Lance, suddenly alert. "C'mon in, I'll call them for you." He led us up a short flight of stairs to the security room overlooking the park, and sat us in chairs. I snuck a peek at Roger and was sorry for him, and also afraid that his appendix would burst in front of me.

"It's hard getting sick when you're away from home," I said, trying to sound like Barb.

"It doesn't matter," said Roger, convincingly. In truth, he looked bored by the whole appendicitis thing. How can you tell when someone really needs support and is just pretending to be fine, versus when someone is fine and is annoyed by you?

I excused myself, feeling cowed, and called Sharon on the landline.

"Should I go with him?" I asked her. "I don't mind," I added quickly.

"No, no. He'll be okay for one night." She spoke gently, in a way I'd never heard before, as if I was the one with appendicitis. She said she'd visit him in the morning, absolving me of responsibility beyond getting him in the ambulance.

The ambulance in question arrived forty-five minutes later from Quesnel, and a kindly middle-aged EMT helped Roger into the vehicle. She began pressing down on different parts of his abdomen.

"Where does it hurt?" she asked.

"Everywhere!" said Roger irritably. She nodded solemnly and scribbled something on her clipboard.

"Bye, Roger," I called from the pavement as the EMT pulled the door shut. I watched the ambulance pull away. There was a sickening sensation in my stomach. It was guilt, and helplessness. I was grateful that I was a middle child, because taking charge in emergencies was exhausting. Reflecting on the experience, I was certain I'd done something horrible in the course of the evening to make things worse, or that there was another way I could have handled things that would reveal itself to me in time.

Back at the cottage, everyone had returned from the bonfire. Riley and John were telling the story of Roger's appendix to a bunch of other residents, their inflections full of drama, careening between deep concern and flagrant indulgence. I told them he went to the hospital, which made them yelp.

Chapter 11

OPENING WEEKEND WAS COLD AND RAINY, AND THERE WERE few visitors. I was both relieved and slightly disappointed by this.

I was in the schoolhouse on my first day. I watched enviously as Agatha pulled on her Edwardian outfit, preparing for a relaxing day in the Wendle House.

"It's actually easier to run the schoolhouse when you have big classes. You'll see," she said. I was still happy there were few people who would watch my first attempt.

My first class of the season was composed of only two families, nine people in total. The children came sprinting across the park when I rang the school bell. I took a big inhale, and began. My voice faltered as I instructed everyone to split into two lines according to gender. I was terrified and wanted to tell everyone to go home, that I was sick. It wasn't until I was halfway through reciting the instructions that I realized the material was inherently delightful, and it didn't truly matter what I said, because forcing someone to wear a bonnet and splay out their fingers for a cleanliness check was a compelling enough psychological experience to sustain interest across the entire length of the hour-long lesson.

"Hmmmm, maybe you ought to have your mother help you with these, uh, after class today," I said to one of the dads, pointing to his dirty fingernails, as Agatha had instructed me to do. I wanted to die, but the tiny class exploded into laughter.

The lesson itself was quite simple. First, I "taught" them how to write in cursive, which most adults knew how to do anyway. For the children, I simply had them copy the example letters on the board, and after a brief demonstration, I had the class mime drawing a cursive capital *A* in the air.

After that, we did a spelling bee, where all the words were related to the British Columbia Gold Rush. Because the school was for kids, the words were easy, like "gold" and "bear."

At the end of class, I made everyone sing "She'll Be Coming 'Round the Mountain." I was supposed to frame this part as a competition, where the boys stood and sang when I raised my right hand, and the girls stood and sang when I raised my left.

I forgot my lines a bunch of times, and there were lots of awkward pauses in my performance, but no one seemed to notice, or if they did, they didn't care. The children squirmed in their seats throughout the lesson, full of excitement and anticipation for the next activity.

"Thank you, Ms. Thompson!" they all recited dutifully as they filed out of class, exhausted from singing.

"Thanks, Miss Thompson!"

"Bye, Mrs. Thompson!" A little girl wrapped her arms around my waist and hugged me. Everyone asked for a photo. I posed awkwardly for their iPhones and pretended not to know what they were. After everyone was gone, I was exhausted. Speaking for almost an hour straight takes a toll on you! I went back into the schoolhouse and sat in one of the cramped desks. I laid my head on the cool wood and closed my eyes. There was a knock at the door. I shot up and spun around to see Daniel in the doorway.

"Wow, you look amazing!" I said. He was wearing his "Reverend Raynard" outfit, consisting of a black floor-length coat overtop of his black habit, and of course, the white collar. He held a cane with a silver head and wore a wide-brimmed black hat with a domed, low crown. He looked like Van Helsing.

"Yours is cool, too!" he said. Daniel was lucky, because, other than Sunday services, he only had one "performance" to do each day: a tour of the cemetery.

"Sharon says no one goes on that tour most of the time. No one showed up today." He explained, not sounding disappointed in the slightest. The rest of the time, he got to wander around the park and talk to people if he wanted to, or just hang out in the back room if there were no guests in the church.

I, on the other hand, had two more classes to get through. They went more or less the same as the first, except for the last class, when a teenage boy asked me if I was going to spank him.

"Um, no?" I said.

Between classes, I put on my bonnet and went up Main Street during a lull in the rain, stopping to watch Ivan hammer a bottle opener into shape at the blacksmith's shop. Up the street, Jeremy was sitting on an overturned barrel and strumming his guitar while two teenage girls watched him, giggling shyly. Farther up the road I could see Min ushering a small group of students into the Chinese schoolhouse for a calligraphy lesson. Toward the end of the afternoon, the park was quiet. I found a romance novel called *Fare Thee Well* in the back room of the schoolhouse.

"A body like that doesn't come around every day," Tug thought, admiring her almost obscene curves as she bent to retrieve her purse.

It had started to rain again by the end of the day. In the change room, I peeled my corset off, revealing bright pink indentations where the plastic boning had pressed into my skin. *A body like this doesn't come around every day*, I recited to myself as I studied myself in the mirror. What was the difference between a body that came around every day and a body that didn't anyway? I tilted my head to watch Agatha, stripping to her underwear across the room. I had no idea how to assess it against my own. Hers was older, and had more wrinkles, but was maybe skinnier than mine. She was shorter than me.

"Now, the first day wasn't so bad, was it?" Agatha said, turning to me and smiling.

"No, it was … fun," I said. We undressed slowly, still acclimating to the jigsaw-like getups Victorian and Edwardian women put on and took off every day. We hung each garment carefully to ensure nothing wrinkled, or tore or got lost.

In the parking lot, I ran into Daniel again, who asked me for a ride home.

"Good day?" I asked.

"Good day," he repeated. I got the sense he might have agreed with anything I had said. Daniel asked me what my plans were that evening.

"I'll probably just try to read a book or something. I never know how to fill my free time when I'm alone," I said.

"Hmmm. I feel that," he said amiably.

"I feel like I'm never taking up hobbies because I worry that, like, someone will want to spend time with me, but they won't be able to find me or access me because I'm doing my hobby," I said, laughing at how stupid that sounded. "It's like my only hobby is being available to other people." I knew that Daniel's agreeableness was tricking me into disclosing more than I had initially meant to. That was a priest's main job, wasn't it? Trying to get people to tell you the private stuff that makes them sad.

"I feel exactly the same way," he said.

"Oh, really?" I said sardonically.

"Yeah, really," he said, emphasizing *really*. "When I was little, I always had a hard time picking up activities, or concentrating on anything. I think I was nervous that someone was looking for me, but I'd never thought about it that way, or said it out loud or anything."

"Maybe our joint summer goal can be to find hobbies and ignore everyone who tries to talk to us. We could learn to skateboard!" I joked.

Daniel laughed. "I would love that," he said. "Do you want to watch a movie tonight or something? I don't have plans either."

"That would be great. We can invite Bobby, too," I added, suddenly worried he thought I was trying to start an affair with him.

At the compound, Bobby, Daniel, and I drank sickly sweet berry ciders and watched the first half of the extended cut of *The Fellowship of the Ring*. We sat crammed together on my bed, so the fabrics of Bobby's and Daniel's shorts rubbed up against my bare legs. We all practised our impressions of Samwise, and Daniel showed us his best Gollum, crouching on the cold compound floor.

"I'm obsessed!" said Bobby, as Daniel clutched an imaginary ring in his hand.

• • •

"I made friends with a boy," I told Barb at our next session.

"Oh, that's great news, Josie," she said.

"He's a priest! And he's married."

Barb laughed. "Well, he sounds like a very safe boy friend for you."

I hadn't thought about it that way.

• • •

After two more days in the schoolhouse, it was my turn to work in the Wendle House. It was an easier time overall. The main idea was to show guests home life in Barkerville during the nineteenth and early twentieth centuries. This mostly consisted of sweeping the floor and making "griddle cakes" in a cast iron pan. The wrought-iron oven was a real pièce de résistance in Barkerville, and I would come to appreciate the fact that I got to work with it multiple times a week. It was enormous, filling about a quarter of the small kitchen. When guests came in, I gave them a long demonstration of its many features.

"And what would I use this for?" I asked a guest, doing my best Agatha impression and resting a hand on the warm iron cupboard suspended above the griddle.

"Um, a bread oven?"

"I should be so lucky! This" — I opened the cupboard to reveal a little cranny with a grated floor — "is what you might call my 'microwave.'" Everyone laughed generously at this comment. I gestured for them to place their hands inside.

"That *is* warm," the tourists said.

"Yes, indeed," I said, nodding sagely. "I can put my supper in here and it will come to the perfect temperature."

People asked lots of dumb questions. "So, you'd probably have like twelve kids by now if you were *really* from the gold rush, right?" one guy asked.

"Um, no," I said. "I don't have any children, and I know lots of women in my day who are waiting to begin families. It might be different for women on farms, or working-class women, though."

"If you say so," he said, unconvinced.

Daniel came to visit me, and I presented him with a slice of my "griddle cake," which was more like a big, family-sized scone.

"Mmmm!" he exclaimed politely.

I made him tea, and as we sat and talked, visitors came in and out, charmed by the wholesome scene we presented.

Agatha had reminded me to bring Ivan a slice of cake to thank him for chopping our wood. I brought him a plate next door at the blacksmith's shop, and he accepted it directly into his blackened hands and took a bite.

"Not bad, not bad," he said, dipping it into his tin mug of coffee. He asked me how I liked being an interpreter.

"It's good, mostly. I don't know that I'm going to be talented at it, though."

"Ah, you're fine."

I asked if he liked being an interpreter.

"I fucking hate it!" he said, pausing for a second to make sure no one had heard him say the f-word. "People coming up to you every day and ask you the same dumb questions. You know, today a guy came up to me and confronted me about my hair, of all things." He gestured to his princely locks. *"You wouldn't really have been allowed to have hair like that, would you?* And I was like what, you think people didn't have hair in the nineteen hundreds? That shut him right up."

"That sounds … annoying. Cool to be a blacksmith, though."

"Oh, it is. You know, blacksmiths traditionally live a lot longer than other people."

"Really?"

"Absolutely. It's the heat." He leaned toward the forge and fanned the hot air into his face. "It's like how the Scandinavians have their hot saunas and stuff. You sweat out all the toxins or something." I couldn't tell if he was teasing me, so I didn't say anything.

Later in the day, Ivan chopped wood for me again. There was something very erotic about watching a guy with sooty hands chop wood for you while you're wearing a corset, and when I was bored in the Wendle House later, I imagined making out with Ivan on his workbench, my white shirt blackening from the soot.

• • •

Barkerville wasn't quiet for long. By the end of the month, crowds were streaming in, having made the long trips from places like Vancouver and Victoria, or Calgary and Edmonton. Suddenly, my classes were thirty or more people. Some people had to stand at the back of the room, pressing their slates against the wall to do their cursive. Crowds moved in and out of each building in droves.

I started to develop responses to the most popular things I'd hear throughout the day.

"Mrs. Thompson! Derek is cheating off me," a woman said about her husband, Derek, who proceeded to pull her hair.

"Now, Miss Morgan, no one likes a tattletale," I said. Everyone laughed.

I noticed that guests at the park operated with a sort of hive mind. Some days, each visitor said the exact same thing.

"Oh! Can you believe the size of this stove?" one guy would say, only for the next visitor to say, "Say, Beth, can you believe the size of this thing?" My task was to come up with the perfect response to these pre-programmed lines for the day.

People were also intensely invested in getting me to admit that I wasn't actually from the past, but was just some twenty-first-century girl with a summer job.

"So, do you live around here?" they'd ask coolly, like they were the good cop and I could tell them the truth.

"Why, yes, I live here in the Wendle House, of course!" I'd say.

"You're good, you're good." They'd chuckle to themselves, as if they'd proven something fundamental about human nature by eliciting this response from me.

Sometimes, men who visited the park told me I was sexy. This was stressful and thrilling, but ultimately hard to take seriously on account of my unnaturally snatched waist. Watching them ogle me, I wanted to say, "Listen, you'd be sexy, too, if you were wearing one of these." I had a sense that I was indulging in something wholly un-feminist. Mostly, I just pretended I didn't hear them, and they all went away eventually.

Daniel told me that men responded to him very differently as an interpreter.

"They definitely don't call me sexy, generally," he said. "I think I scare the shit out of them."

"What?" I was confused. Nothing about Daniel was scary.

"Well, their wives and mothers seem to love me. But the men don't know what to do with me. I confuse them, I think. I'm not 'manly,' you know, and I'm supposed to be sensitive and a good listener by nature of my profession. They do anything they can to avoid talking to me or coming face-to-face with me. They hide behind their wives!" He didn't sound hurt by this. He didn't seem to care.

This phenomenon fascinated me, and I told Agatha what Daniel had said.

"That makes perfect sense," she said. "It frightens them to see a man who is comfortable being vulnerable. Plus, he's got those movie-star good looks."

No one had ever described Daniel as having "movie-star good looks" to me before, but the more I considered it I realized she wasn't wrong. He did have a certain striking quality to his appearance, and a pleasant way of holding his face when he wasn't speaking. Attractiveness could be so mysterious. Sometimes you saw that someone was attractive right away, and other times it snuck up on you and scared you.

I wondered what Louisa looked like. I pictured her, delicate but strong and extremely beautiful, bowing her cello furiously. I pulled out my phone, but put it back in my pocket without typing her name into the Facebook search bar, wanting to preserve the mystery.

As time went on, I was learning the unique power the school-teacher position afforded me, in the classroom at least. I had to treat everyone like a little kid, and people mostly loved it and slipped into it easily, happy to have a break from the outside world of decision-making. They performed their roles eagerly, raising their hands and grinning at me as I praised them.

The ones who hated it were the dads, some of whom seemed physically incapable of humbling themselves in this way, and the teenagers, who were trying so hard to distance themselves from their childhoods.

The secret, I came to understand, was "She'll Be Coming 'Round the Mountain." For the people who liked the schoolhouse, it was a fun way to end the lesson. For the people who hated it, it was an opportunity for me to force them to submit to my will, disarming them with levity and song. I made them stand, and sit, and stand and sit again, barking at them to sing louder, louder! By the end of the last verse, even my strongest detractors were sweaty and smiling despite themselves, and offered me shy bows and "thank you, Mrs. Thompson"s as they exited the classroom.

• • •

In my role as an authority figure, as camp caretaker, in the real world, things were not going as smoothly. At the compound, Roger was back and had recovered from his surgery. He and Riley and John now found it funny to sit down on the flimsy kitchen chairs with as much of their weight as possible to see whether the chairs could bear the pressure. They managed to break five of them before Bobby clued me into it.

"We don't do that," Roger said flatly when I confronted them, staring pointedly past me at John, who was leaning against the kitchen counter. They'd managed to attract more members to their clique, and together they regularly decorated the kitchen for increasingly elaborate themed parties. That week, it was "Under the Sea," and Riley had put a temporary tattoo of a fish on her cheek.

"Looks cool in here," I said. The sinks were overflowing with dishes. The counters were smeared with unknown foodstuffs and stained with coffee. My positive encouragement surrounding cleanliness had not yielded results, and I was starting to run out of ideas. "Don't forget though to, uh, do your dishes and take your stuff from the common space when you leave."

"Um, I think we're all super clean," said Roger, turning on "Old Town Road." "This place is so dreary. They should be thanking us for brightening it up."

"Oh, definitely," I said. "Just something to keep in mind … the bowls in the sink, for example."

"Well, those are soaking," said Roger. They were definitely not soaking.

"Okay, well, it's important that other people have space to cook, so just make sure it's done before bed if they're yours."

"Um, yeah, of course?" said Roger, aggression creeping into his voice. I thought he was being an asshole.

"Have an awesome night!" I said as I left.

"Byyeeeeee," recited the group. I could hear laughter behind me as I returned to my room.

In the mornings, Greg would come to say hello to me on his way to the Richfield Courthouse. He'd lean against the school-house gate as I raised the flag and tell me about the books he was reading.

"The birds!" he called to me one morning as he passed by.

"Huh?" I said.

"The birds! Daphne du Maurier wrote 'The Birds'!" He was referring to a conversation we had had the week prior, where neither of us could remember the one famous thing she had written, aside from *Rebecca*.

"Oh my God, that's it!" I said. I had a crush on Greg. I imagined him as my boyfriend, with his arm around me at a restaurant or a bonfire with the other judges. I would tuck his stringy hair behind his ear as I'd watch him make a joke, and not mind that he was a little bit strange looking. In fact, I'd like it, because it would mean he'd belong to me, and not the rest of the world.

My crush on Greg felt different from many of my previous crushes because he was available, and not out of my league, and seemed to like me. Was I finally finished chasing after things and people who want nothing to do with me and were out of my league? Was I finally ready to want the things that want me, and nothing more? For the first time in a long time, romantic fulfillment felt within my grasp.

Creak creak, I thought to myself, remembering Barb's story about opening her heart.

"Oh my God, I had a nightmare about you!" Logan said on our drive to Quesnel. "I had a dream that *Greg* asked you out. I was like 'girl, run.'"

"Oh my God, that's so nuts!" I said, turning red.

"To be honest I would *not* be surprised if he did. He seems kind of obsessed with you. Isn't he always visiting you at work? Be caaaareful. He's so … weird." She did a little shiver. I beamed, both because Logan believed he liked me and because she saw me as the type of girl a guy could become "obsessed with."

"Definitely. Super weird," I said.

• • •

To my surprise, Barb didn't have much to say about my new crush.

"Well, I hope that you learn a lot from this experience. A crush can be fun." She sounded almost bored. She waxed poetic in her usual way, but said nothing more on the subject. Wasn't she the one who wanted me to get a boyfriend so bad? I didn't bring it up again after that, afraid she would say something terrible, like I wasn't actually ready for a boyfriend, or that I was being pathetic.

I didn't care if Barb wasn't excited for me, I was excited enough for both of us. Greg and I had been doing our little routine for weeks, and it was maybe going to happen for me, finally. After years of mismatched crushes and disappointments, it was finally working out. I fantasized about the weeks to come if things went my way, with a boyfriend by my side, a peaceful mind.

In my fantasy, Daniel was always there, too, and sometimes Bobby and the other judges, watching Greg and me hold hands as we strolled down Main Street, caught up in an engaging conversation.

There was a big staff party at the Wake-Up Jake for Canada Day, or "Dominion Day" as we called it at Barkerville for historical accuracy. I was sure something was going to happen between Greg and me.

By this part of summer, the air was warm enough during the day, but it was full of little gnats that swarmed noisily through the air, leaving microscopic red bites all over any exposed skin. When Bobby, Daniel, and I arrived at the Jake, a crowd of interpreters and curatorial staff were standing outside the doors, passing around bug spray. We closed our eyes and held our breath as we sprayed any skin that was left exposed to the flies.

"Don't spray it on your leggings," Sharon warned me. "It dissolves them."

"It gives you cancer," said Henrick sternly, who was not wearing any bug spray. He was fidgety, trying not to scratch at his ankles and neck.

"I mean, it's one time," said Brandon while liberally spraying Ailish, who held her breath and closed her eyes.

That night, everyone really let loose. Bobby drank five beers by my count, and she kissed me on both cheeks before enticing Mike onto the dance floor with her to do the macarena. I even saw Hannah and Armand swaying conservatively together near the back of the room. I found myself a seat at a table that faced Greg directly, and I watched him laughing with his friends and waited for him to look up at me.

Daniel was watching me, and I pretended not to notice. Suddenly, Greg turned his head, and our eyes met. He looked disconcerted when he saw me, and he averted his gaze quickly, turning his attention markedly to Millie Saunders, who had just recently graduated high school, and to Henrick.

I was confused, and my body was suddenly hot, even though it was only eighteen degrees Celsius outside. Something had gone very wrong, and I could tell, without needing any more information, that he was not interested in me, and possibly never had been. I thought about all the times Greg and I had spoken, and tried to figure out what was going on. Daniel caught my gaze, his eyes kind. The idea that he could glean what was going on in my head was troubling to me. I jolted out of my seat, abandoning him, and joined Bobby, Mike, and Logan on the dance floor. I tried to focus on the music and have fun, but my eyes kept drifting over to Greg, who wouldn't look at me again.

After that night, Greg didn't visit me anymore. At first, he'd wave politely as he passed by on his journey to the courthouse, but then he stopped altogether, speed-walking beyond my line of vision as I raised the flag and opened the shutters. I started avoiding the judges altogether, afraid they had all been discussing my crush, which now seemed obvious to everyone around me. Surely everyone knew, and had discussed my value, or lack thereof, and that's why Greg had decided not to talk to me anymore.

I told Barb about this at my next appointment.

"I think ... I think Greg doesn't like me anymore," I said, and promptly burst into tears. They were the big, fat tears of a disappointed child. "I just ... I just," I blubbered, wiping my nose with the sleeve my sweater. Barb handed me a box of tissues. "I just *thought ...*"

"Yeah," Barb said softly. I cried more. I had cried in front of Barb many times, but this was a different kind of crying. I surprised and almost impressed myself with the heaving wails that left my body. Evidently, I was upset about Greg. I had been disappointed in love many times in my life, but I had not cried about a man like this in many years.

I started again, when I could talk. "I guess I just thought I had figured things out. I always feel like I'm picking the wrong things, and that's why I'm alone all the time, and so messed up. I thought that Greg wasn't too good for me, and that he would like me. I thought he did like me." I started sobbing again. "But not even he likes me. Everyone else gets to pick what they want, but I can't. No one wants me. Not even Greg." My throat was getting sore.

"Mhmmmmm," said Barb, making her listening face. I blew my nose loudly.

"I have no value."

"Everyone has value, Josie," said Barb. "No matter who does and who doesn't want to go out with you."

"It doesn't matter how much value I have anyway, if no one sees it. It's all hypothetical until someone sees it."

"Maybe you can recognize your own value?" said Barb. I ignored her.

"And why am I so obsessed with men?" I said, raising my voice. "It's boring! Where is my character? I just wish someone would tell me what I have to do to have a normal relationship with the world around me. I just wish someone would teach a class on how to fit in with everything." I sighed heavily, suddenly very tired. "I guess I just wish I had the skills," I said.

"The skills?"

"You know, skills to get the people I like to like me. Or to get men to like me. I feel like I have no control over what happens to me, or who I'm thrown together with. It's random for me, but obviously some people know how to do it, but no one will tell me."

"Hmmm," said Barb. "So, you want someone to tell you how they get people to like them?"

"Yeah!"

"Do you wanna know what I do?" said Barb, a wicked twinkle appearing in her eye.

"What?"

"Or, used to do before I got married, I should say."

"Um, yeah, I guess." I couldn't believe this. Usually when people were married or had a boyfriend, they pretend they didn't do anything special to make their partner like them. But I always knew they did, and Barb was going to tell me.

"So when I lived in Vancouver, there was this bar I'd go to with my friends, and there were always the cutest guys there for some reason. That was like its thing."

"Okay."

"And basically, if there was one I liked, I'd do this thing. I'd look at him, really intensely." She mimed staring, or rather, glaring, across the room at an imaginary cute guy. "Then, he'd notice eventually and look back. Our eyes would meet, and I'd look away, and not look back."

"Okay," I said.

"Then, after a few minutes, I'd do it again." She mimed looking up again. "Usually, he'd already be looking, but if he wasn't he'd always look back in a second or two. After that, usually they'd approach me."

"Seriously?"

"Every time."

"That's what you did."

"That's what I did."

I wanted to laugh, but I appreciated that we had both just made very vulnerable admissions to one another in the last hour, and she'd given me potentially explosive intel into the dating world.

"Well, thank you for telling me, Barb."

"Try it sometime, maybe something great will happen."

"Maybe I will." I suppressed a snicker.

"You know, it's possible this guy had something else going on," Barb said after a pause. "Maybe this guy wasn't right for you, and now you have space for something, or someone, else in your life. Someone who does like you back."

"I guess." I sighed.

I felt better immediately after I left her office. Out in the mild Quesnel air, Greg wasn't so interesting to me anymore, and by the time I arrived at Granville's Coffee at the end of Main Street, I couldn't remember what I'd liked so much about him, and why I had been so upset. Already, the girl who had liked Greg was gone. But who replaced her?

I was so lucky that there was someone in my life whose job was to listen to me say embarrassing and terrible things, and she legally wasn't allowed to tell anyone unless I committed a crime. In my mind, this was incentive enough to never commit a crime.

I was meeting Daniel at Granville's Coffee. Logan was working overtime that week on a project for Charles, so I'd asked if he wanted to come. I was ravenous, and ordered a shepherd's pie that was smothered in cheese. Daniel didn't order anything, but he politely watched me eat, and didn't comment on how splotchy my face was from my session with Barb.

"Can I ask you a question?" I said to Daniel as I spooned a heap of ground beef into my mouth.

"Shoot." He sounded nervous, like I might ask him for a kidney.

"What do you like about Louisa?" I was feeling nihilistic, and after Barb's admission, I was in the mood to ask probing questions about the nature of love and attraction.

Daniel took a second. "That's a nice question. I think she's … intense."

"She's intense?" When I imagined what a man wanted in a girlfriend or wife, intense was lower on the list of qualities I could name.

"Yeah, she gets really into stuff, and she really cares about the things she does. It's exciting, and really … brave," he said. "And, of course, she's beautiful, and I love so many things about her."

For a minute, I had a strong urge to lead Daniel back to Barb's office and introduce him to her. "Look!" I'd say. "Look at this nice man!"

"That's beautiful, Daniel," I said.

"I'm so anxious all the time," he continued. "She gives me confidence."

"I'm anxious all the time, too," I admitted. "That must be nice."

Daniel told me that when he was little, he was so anxious all the time that he developed these intrusive thoughts. "Couldn't get rid of them. Horrible, stressful ones, like violent stuff."

"That's terrible. When I was little, I had a similar thing. Less intense, obviously. I developed these tics. I blinked my eyes really hard a few times a minute for a few years. It really freaked my mom out. She thought I had a brain tumour. When I think back, I was obviously just stressed out of my mind."

"People always tell me that I make them feel so calm when I'm with them, that I'm a calming presence. It bugs me, because I'm always stressed out," he said. We were both grinning.

"People say that to me, too. They say I'm so 'happy-go-lucky,' or bubbly, whatever, but I think it's just my face."

"If only they knew," Daniel said.

"Maybe I'll marry someone who gives me confidence, like you did," I said.

"I think that's a good instinct. It's served me well. She's visiting at the end of August, you know. I can't wait for you to meet, I think she'll love you." The thought of Daniel thinking about me and determining that Louisa would love me almost made me forget how alone I had felt only an hour ago.

"I can't wait to meet her," I said. "Ow." A piece of shepherd's pie burned the roof of my mouth.

Chapter 12

EVERY DAY, I FELT BETTER, AND I WAS HAPPIER THAT I hadn't shared my crush with anyone but Barb. When I saw Greg around Barkerville after that trip to Quesnel, eating a pickled egg outside the Wake-Up Jake, or making a loud joke to his friends, he now seemed slovenly, and not likeable at all. I could not believe I had wanted him to kiss me, and I began to consider myself lucky that he hadn't.

I was feeling stronger, but my suffering was not quite over. Things at the compound were getting out of hand, and quickly. The kitchen had devolved into madness. The tables and ceilings were strewn with leftover decorations from the increasingly elaborate themed parties that Roger and his gang hosted. The sinks and counters were downright disgusting some days, and three residents had come to complain to me, begging me to do something. Sharon and I implemented a "three strikes" policy.

I issued a strike to Jason, an intern at Island Mountain Arts, for refusing to buy Tupperware and instead using the pots and pans to store his food.

"Everyone else needs those to cook!" I told him.

"I don't know why we can't all take care of our own shit," he said, glaring defiantly at the slip of paper I handed him, as if he might rip it up and throw it in my face. "I don't think other people should be controlling how I store my food."

"This is getting scary. Like, it's kind of fucked up to demand perfection from people when it comes to tasks like keeping spaces clean," Riley said. "It's pretty ableist, actually?"

"Well, everyone who lives in the camp signed a contract indicating that they would keep their spaces clean. It's not fair to everyone else who uses the kitchen," I said.

Riley looked at me like I had said that babies can be a delicious snack if properly prepared. "Right," she said.

I had been bad at doing my dishes when I was in my teens and early twenties, too, but I always felt guilty about it, even years later. I thought Riley must have been a very confident person if she truly thought it was fucked up to make her do her dishes. It was impressive, even if I did think she was a little bit evil. I found myself comparing her unfavourably to Hannah, who always did her dishes.

Frustrated and stressed, I went to the pub. There, I ran into Janine, who offered me a listening ear.

"Managing a living space can be tough," she said, tilting her head sympathetically.

I explained to her about the three strikes, and how I had tried to be gentle at first, but it wasn't working. "It's a bit stressful," I said. "I hope I can figure something out."

As I said this, her face changed, as it often did, into a big scowl.

"Well, you're *never* going to make any headway with these people, Josie. You know why?"

"What?" As usual, her shift in tone threw me off balance.

"You messed up from the beginning. You messed up by being soft on them," she said.

"Oh," I said. "Well —"

"No," she said, raising her eyebrows and shaking her head. "No, Josie. You have to set firm rules from the *beginning*." She chuckled to herself then, as if marvelling at how smart she was, and how stupid I was.

"You know what, Janine? I think it's *fine*," I said, my voice cutting through the background chatter of the pub.

"Well —" she said. I cut her off.

"No, if I fuck up, who cares? Have you never made a mistake? Jesus!"

Janine looked genuinely taken aback. "You know, you have a point, you have a point," she said quickly, now nodding with intensity to show me she was seriously taking this new data into account.

"You know what? I have to go," I said, rising from my chair. "See ya, Janine. Thanks for the talk."

"Good luck!" she called after me, meekly.

. . .

"I feel guilty about being salty to Janine," I said to Barb.

"Do you?" she said. "It doesn't sound like you said anything that bad."

"I do feel bad," I said. "But, really, how does everyone move through life with so much … confidence? Everyone thinks they're so smart."

"Some people do," Barb said. Barb would never admit to an absolute.

"Why don't I have that?"

"I don't know, why don't you?"

Bobby, Daniel, and I had started watching *Mad Men* together in the evenings after work. We agreed that Betty was unfairly maligned and misunderstood, despite her flaws, and that Daniel was like Pete Campbell, if he were more likeable. Bobby did a funny dance to the theme song where she swung her arms in circles. Daniel and I swayed our arms above our heads as she danced.

Recently, though, Bobby had been skipping out on our nightly viewing appointments to spend time with Mike and Marcia, the senior summer curatorial assistant.

"I'm at Mike's. Go ahead, I'll catch up on my own," she'd message our group chat, or "I'm with Marcia and Mike, we're going to Bowron. Don't wait up!"

At first, Daniel and I decided not to watch without her, and instead we'd have a bonfire behind the compound, or he'd call Louisa and I'd read a book. But then, we grew impatient.

"I want to find out what happens!" Daniel said as he pressed play on my laptop, his voice slightly whiny. "We can't wait forever." I was amused by his petulance, but also ecstatic that he liked something I'd introduced him to, and that he was revealing a more secret, less agreeable part of himself to me after all this time. We continued watching together, meeting almost every night. When my favourite parts approached, I would turn my head slightly to see his reaction.

Bobby used to invite Daniel and me to have breakfast at the Wake-Up Jake before work with Mike and Marcia, but she'd been doing it less and less lately.

"It annoys Marcia so much when I invite you guys," she admitted to me. We were in the schoolhouse on a quiet day. I was wiping slates, and she was taking a break from weeding the cemetery, leaning her head back on the seat of a desk.

"What?" I said.

"Yeah, she's always like 'you didn't tell me that Josie and Daniel were coming.'" Bobby did an impression of Marcia's gruff voice.

"Does she not like us or something?" At this, Bobby shrugged, her smirk playing on her lips. I didn't press her. I didn't think about Marcia all that much. When I pictured her, I just pictured her big dog, and her short, cropped grey hair, and her slightly menacing laugh. The idea that she might have private, negative opinions about me was frightening, so I tried not to think about it.

Bobby visited me a lot at work. I fed her chocolate cake from the wrought-iron stove, and we sat in the hammock beside the Wendle House together, watching whistle pigs beg tourists for pieces of their lunch. We'd mutter pieces of gossip we'd heard around town to each other and complain about the people that irritated us. I told her about what Janine had said about the compound.

"Bitch," she said.

"Right?"

Talking with her was intoxicating. But sometimes, after she'd gone, I experienced a guilty, sickly pang in my stomach, like I'd eaten too much of something sweet. I was used to keeping my more horrible thoughts inside, or expressing them in the safety of Barb's office, where I knew they'd stay private. Was I infecting the collective psyche of Wells and Barkerville by expressing these thoughts to Bobby? What if she told Marcia? I reminded myself that I should trust her to be discreet about the things I say, because she was my friend, and because she was always forthcoming with me in return.

The next week Bobby, flustered, came to see me in the Wendle House.

"What is it?" I asked. Her cheeks were flushed, but she still held that ironic expression on her face, as if she were just blushing at an in-joke with herself.

"Well ... I have something to tell you," she said. She adopted a lilting, girlier tone to her voice as she said this. "Don't be mad at me, promise?"

"Huh?" I said. That made me a little bit mad at her. "Of course, I won't be mad at you. What's going on?"

"Well," she said, smiling bigger now, "Mike and I are in love."

"What?" I said. I had not been expecting that, and yet, as she said it, it made some sense. Their interactions, in hindsight, were so explosive and passionate, and they were always arguing about one thing or another.

"I know," she said. "It's shocking."

"Well, what happened?"

"So, we went canoeing on Bowron last night, right? And Mike and I have always, you know, razzed each other a lot, it's normal for us." She explained their flirtation to me like a nuclear physicist might explain a breakthrough theorem to a group of graduate students. "Well, lately, things have just felt ... different between us." She narrowed her eyes dramatically.

"Hmmm ..." I said.

"So last night, we're fucking around, getting the canoe into the water. And he keeps making this joke about how he 'stole my heart.' So funny, right? 'Oh, I totally stole your heart this summer, didn't I?' and at one point I just had to stop, and be like, what are we *really* talking about here? And that's when everything happened."

"What ... happened?" I asked, stupidly.

"Well, you know, we told each other everything. How we'd been feeling about each other. It was all so overwhelming." She stared past me with a dreamy gaze, no doubt remembering the private things they'd said to each other. "Then later we ... you know."

"Oh," I said. I tried to look happy for her, even though I felt like I had missed a step on the stair. At the beginning of the summer, neither of us had ever had a boyfriend, or had sex with a man.

Now, at twenty-two, Bobby was taking those steps without me, and moving on to a new stage of life, where things I didn't know about, or understand, took place. And she had held these feelings secretly. I had, too, about Greg, I realized, but that didn't soften the sting.

"Listen, I hope you're not upset," Bobby said a few seconds later. "Mike told me you have a crush on him."

"*What?*" I shouted. Out the open window, a flock of startled cowbirds took flight. "No! Of course, I don't."

"Okie doke!" said Bobby, her voice falsely cheerful. I had protested too much, and now Bobby had replaced her open, happy face with her aloof one. I fought the urge to keep talking, to tell her I thought Mike was ridiculous, and I would never like someone like him.

"I'm happy for you," I said instead.

"Thanks," she said.

I was in a bad mood for the rest of the day and into the next morning. I kept imagining the moment that Mike told Bobby he thought I had a crush on him, trying to picture what exactly he would have said, and how he'd have said it. How long had Bobby and I been spending time together, making jokes, all while she believed I had unrequited feelings for Mike? Did they feel sorry for me? Were they laughing at me? I remembered how in some movies, characters would say "I'm so mad I could spit." I tried spitting into the sink in the compound bathroom. It didn't make me any less angry.

It was my day off. In the kitchen, I saw John had made boxed mac and cheese the night before, as he often did. He'd left the saucepan on the stove, as he always did, with an inch of water and dried cheese sauce sticking to the sides. I sighed.

Issuing strikes had improved the conditions of the kitchen overall, but there was a new hostility in my relations with some of the residents. Riley sometimes muttered "fascist" under her breath as she passed me in the halls.

The previous week, I had asked John to end a phone call. It was 11:00 p.m., and his voice was reverberating down the serrated metal hallway. Bobby, whose workday began at five thirty, messaged me on Facebook: "Can you *please* make him stop?"

"Gotta go, Mom," he said, sounding frightened as I approached him.

"Thanks so much, John, you can talk tomorrow. A lot of the residents have to get up pretty early, so they need to sleep." He didn't say anything, scuffling to his feet and back to his room wordlessly.

"You know," Riley had called to me across the kitchen when she saw me the next day, "could you just, maybe, think about how these 'rules' you enforce affect the mental health of the residents here?" She had marched across the room and now stood squarely in front of me, hands on her hips. She was a lot shorter than me. Up close, I could see her dreadlocks had made progress.

"Um," I said.

"You know, John is really homesick," she said. She almost had tears in her eyes. "*Really homesick.* And the idea that he can't call his mother has been so hard for him. Because of you. Do you know that the hallway is the only place he gets reception on his cell phone?" She was so angry. My hands were shaking.

"Um, well, he can talk to his mother if he wants to, just not at eleven o'clock in the hallway."

"Listen, all I'm asking" — she paused again — "all I'm asking is that you consider the mental health of the people living here." She stood between me and the door for a minute, as if trying to decide whether she'd say more. She eventually left, shaking her head as she went. I went to my room and threw my phone at the wall.

Now, faced with John's dirty dishes, I wasn't sure if I had the strength to enforce the rules. Nonetheless, I knocked on his door.

Roger, who was leaving his room down the hall, called to me. "John's at work."

I drove to Barkerville. I didn't want to leave a strike for John at his door. Besides, I needed to pick up my cheque anyway.

In the confectionary shop, I found John behind the counter.

"Oh, hey, John, how are you?" I asked him.

"Um, I'm fine."

"I just, um, wanted to remind you to make sure to do your dishes. Can you make sure you do them when you get home?" I could feel the overly cheerful expression on my face. My lip trembled from the effort of it. John didn't say anything, and studied the counter.

"Um, I just wanted to remind you to do your dishes, okay?" I repeated.

"Is that … a threat?" he asked quietly.

"Of course not!" I said. "I just wanted to *remind* you."

"Actually, I've been reading the rent agreement," he continued. "You're not allowed to talk to me about disciplinary matters outside of the compound, and especially not while I'm at work." He paused. "It's harassment," he added quietly.

"Oh, yeah. You're right," I said. Technically, the rules did say that. "I guess I didn't think of this as disciplinary."

"I think it's best you leave," said John, his expression withering. I obeyed him, and went directly to St. Saviour's. As I'd hoped, I found Daniel.

"Yikes," said Daniel when I told him what had happened. "John sucks."

"You think so?" I asked. I pressed my forehead against a cool pew.

"Of course," Daniel said. "Every morning when I have my breakfast, the only time I have to myself before I have to talk to people all day, he comes and sits with me and asks me questions about God. It's so annoying." This made me laugh. "And that cowboy hat. No, he's just being shitty." I was relieved. If Daniel thought John was wrong, and annoying, it must be true.

Daniel and I agreed that, to cover my ass, I should tell Sharon what happened.

"John actually already paid me a visit," she said from behind her desk when I went to visit her the next day. My heart sank. I must have looked pretty upset because she smiled warmly at me, which I'd never seen her do to anyone.

"He was ... emphatic in his arguments, but it doesn't sound like you did anything all that wrong. Maybe just keep compound discussions on the compound from now on. It's no big deal, I promise."

"I'm sorry," I said. Was it possible I had actually traumatized John, and Sharon was protecting me?

"You're fine, don't worry," she said. "I think, though, getting a handle on the residents has been difficult for you?"

"I ..." I trailed off. "Yes, it's been hard. I'm sorry, I'm not good at this." I stopped myself before I said "I'm sorry" again.

"I think it's the procedure to blame, not you. This is the first year we've even had the compound, so we didn't know what to expect at all."

"I dunno, Sharon."

"We should have prepared you better. We're going to fix it."

• • •

Sharon called all the residents into the kitchen for a meeting. Bobby wasn't there, she was hiking with Mike and Marcia, but I wished she was.

"We wanted to have this general meeting to check in about the state of the camp common spaces, and just to have a discussion about how things are going here," said Sharon, standing in the doorway. She was making a professional face, and her voice was level, like a newscaster. Dougie stood behind her, nodding in agreement with everything she said. My hands were so sweaty.

Roger raised his hand. "We have something to say!"

"Well, I was going to go over some talking points first, but you go ahead."

Roger stood and pulled a piece of lined paper out of his pocket. He unfolded it and began to read.

"We, as rent-paying residents at this compound, have been subject to unfair treatment and intimidation. Namely, Josie has consistently crossed professional boundaries, and her interactions with residents have been especially hostile. We have seen this when she threatened John at his place of work. This has been one incident in a long line of misconduct. We consider this a serious breach of trust. We do not feel safe with her in her current role, and we recommend her removal."

I was having trouble regulating my breathing, and each exhale became more and more scraggly. Roger finished his speech, and his eyes darted around the room nervously. Riley sat beside him, her face triumphant and proud. I could hear her voice in the writing.

"Okay," Sharon said, her voice genial. "So, a few of you feel this way?" Was Sharon actually having this meeting to hold me accountable for my conduct as the caretaker? Had I walked into a horrible trap?

"Well, me, Riley, John, of course, and also Deena and Marcus have signed off on this. We've all been witness to her bad behaviour."

"Well, you're right it's important not to discuss compound matters at work." She smiled at Roger the way you might at a child explaining their love of dinosaurs. "But I believe John has already brought that to my attention, and I consider the issue resolved."

"We, uh, feel this matter is of the utmost importance," said Roger.

"Josie, do you have any response to this?" asked Sharon.

I rose from my chair. My legs didn't feel like legs at all; they didn't feel like anything. "Um, well," I began. My face was already twisted into some shape or another in an effort to prevent tears from escaping my eyes. "I think I've done my best so far, and I'm sorry if communication has not been ... um, good." I stopped, unsure of what else to say. "If anyone ever has a problem with a strike or anything else I am always available to ... speak ... to." Hot tears ran down my face, and I sat back down. Daniel, sitting in the chair beside me, patted me lightly on the back.

"Thank you, Josie," Sharon said, with reverence. She blinked her eyes at me, like a cat saying "I love you."

I couldn't hear the rest of Sharon's discussion. My lip drew itself downward, and my eyes dripped tears that slowed directly into my mouth and nose. I pushed my chair away from the table noisily and left the meeting, feeling everyone's eyes on my back. I went to my room. I replayed Roger's speech over and over in my head. *Especially hostile ... we do not feel safe ... long line of misconduct ...*

I heard a knock at the door. Everyone already knew I was crying, so I opened it.

Daniel was holding two tall cans of beer.

"Can I join you?" he asked gingerly. I nodded and moved aside. He opened one of the cans and passed it to me before opening his own.

"Thanks," I said, before starting to sob again.

"You did a good job, Josie. I'm proud of you."

"Thanks, Daniel." I blew my nose on a stray roll of toilet paper.

"Those people are young, and stupid. Sharon knows you're trying to make the compound better for everyone, and you're just doing your job. The kids don't see that yet." I wanted to lean my head against his shoulder and go to sleep.

"It's just that I'm so bad at everything." I was sobbing again. "It's so embarrassing."

"I don't think you're embarrassing."

"I think it is," I said quietly. I knew I was being dramatic, and pathetic, but I didn't care. I didn't think Daniel would care. "I was stupid to think I could do this."

"You are doing it, though," Daniel said. "You just needed some help. We all do."

"Daniel?" I said.

"Yeah?"

"I bet you're a great priest," I said, laughing.

"Thanks, Josie." We drank our beers, and Daniel listened to me complain about the residents.

"Why is Riley so scary? And Roger? I sat with him when he had appendicitis, and *this* is how he repays me?" I said, leaning into my indignance. Daniel laughed.

There was another knock at the door. This time it was Sharon.

"Jesus Christ!" Sharon said. "That was one of the craziest meetings I've ever facilitated, and I've facilitated a lot of meetings." She was in a good mood.

"Awww," she said when she saw me. "It's okay!" She gave me a stiff hug. Daniel got her a beer.

Sharon told us that she told them that the camp would get shut down if they didn't do their dishes because of health codes, and then they'd be homeless.

"That shut them up," she said. "That Roger is a piece of work, isn't he?"

I beamed at her.

Bobby found the three of us an hour later, sitting on my bed and laughing, when she returned from hiking. She made a face when she saw I had been crying.

"Um, something happened?" Sharon and Daniel let me tell the story.

"Well, yikes! Sorry I skipped it, Sharon," she said, not sounding sorry at all.

Sharon left, and then it was time for Daniel to go, too. I didn't want him to leave, but I knew it was too late to start a movie or an episode of something. I let him go and could hear his footsteps fading down the hall and his heavy door slamming shut.

After therapy in Quesnel the next week, I went to Books and Company with Logan. While browsing the shelves, I came face to face with Greg.

"Oh!" I said. "Hi!"

I was invested in being friendly to Greg because I didn't want him to think I was obsessed with him. On the other hand, I didn't want to be too friendly, because I didn't want him to think I was obsessed with him.

"Heyyo," he said, avoiding my eye and instead looking at the books behind me with determination.

"How's it going? Is it your weekend?"

"Um, yeah! What are you doing in town?"

"Oh, I just had therapy." I liked telling people I was in therapy because I got to talk about Barb, which I loved doing. "Now I'm looking for a book."

"Oh, therapy, nice," he said, relaxing a little. I must have been doing a good job acting not obsessed with him. "Is your therapist good? Who do you see?"

"Oh, um, I see Barb. Barbara Sharpe?" I said. "Are you looking for a therapist?"

"Oh, um, no. Barb is my therapist, too."

"She is?" My hands went numb.

"Yeah," he said. Based on the panicked expression that had come over his face, I thought his hands might be numb, too.

"She's the best," I said, after a minute.

"She really is," he replied. I laughed because I didn't know what else to do. We stared at each other. I seriously considered leaving town forever.

"So, are you looking for any book in particular?" I said.

"Yeah, Millie" — he gestured to the couches at the back of the store, where I saw Millie Saunders sipping a beverage from a mug — "she told me about this book she really wants, it's about transcendental meditation, so ... I'm going to buy it for her."

"Oh, why?" I asked. I thought maybe she had mowed his lawn or something.

"Um, because she's an incredible human being?" he said brusquely.

"Oh, yeah, of course." Neither of us said anything.

"Well, see you," he said, a bit coldly.

"Yeah, see you around." I tried to sound cheerful.

"I had such a weird conversation with Greg," I said to Logan in the car.

"Oh, yeah. He was in there with Millie Saunders, right?" said Logan. "Brandon says they're dating."

"Wait, they're going out? Isn't she, like, seventeen?"

"She turned eighteen in April." Logan said, snickering. "Brandon was extra careful to point that out to me."

"Oh," I said.

Chapter 13

AFTER EVERYTHING THAT HAD HAPPENED AT THE COMPOUND, I was overjoyed that Logan and I had scheduled a trip for the next week. I wanted nothing more than to leave Wells for a while.

We were going to Banff for five days. We'd talked about it and booked the time off in April, before I'd even started my job. That felt like a million years ago now. So much had happened to me without Logan. I wasn't even volunteering with the fire department anymore, and we were making separate plans to go to Quesnel more often than not, due to our different schedules in the summer. I wasn't sure how we would fit together now.

Still, Logan ran out of the staff house, positively gleeful, as I pulled into the driveway.

"I'm so exciiiiiiiited!" she said, and wrapped me into a big, clunky car-seat hug.

Her warmth and enthusiasm reminded me that I loved Logan and that she had been a joy in my life. Why hadn't I remembered that? Where was my sense of loyalty?

The drive to Banff was nine hours. We took turns driving while the other napped in the passenger seat, or else discussed happenings around Wells and Barkerville.

We left Wells early, but ended up arriving in Banff well after nightfall, starving and exhausted. We tried five restaurants before we were seated for dinner in a divey place in the basement unit underneath a much nicer restaurant and ate tiny fried chicken burgers with McCain's fries on the side. We checked into our hostel with an Australian desk clerk, and collapsed into creaky bunk beds.

In reality, we only had three days to visit, because we'd spend the last day driving back, so we kept things simple. We visited Lake Louise, which was overcrowded and noisy, and balked at the $90 fee to rent a canoe. I thought of Bowron Lake, and how we could have just stayed in Wells and used Bobby's canoe for free. The only difference was the hue of the water, I was sure. At least Bowron was quiet.

"The water *is* nice," I said.

"It is," Logan agreed.

We did a popular, well-trodden hike to a place called Lower Falls. We hiked as part of a long procession of tourists, which took the special feeling out of the whole thing. The group of teens in front of us held a portable speaker and played Top 40 hits. When we arrived at the falls, a young woman with white-blond hair asked us to take a photo of her. She posed in a way that made her legs look long and her breasts more prominent. She flashed a peace sign.

Her name was Letitia, and she was travelling solo from Missouri, where she worked as a nurse. She was engaged and showed us her giant princess-cut diamond ring.

Logan really liked Letitia and invited her to have dinner with us. We went to a restaurant that was all fondue and was outfitted like a luxe retro log cabin. Logan, eager as I wasn't to try exotic meats, ordered a spread for herself with bison, boar, and venison. I had chicken and beef.

"You sure you don't want to try some, Josie?" asked Logan, waving her skewer in front of me. "I thought you weren't eating meat anyway?"

"Oh … yeah, I kind of dropped that for now." A few weeks ago, while drunk at the pub with Bobby, I had ordered a cheeseburger that I found so delicious that I ate another one the very next day.

Each table had a phone with which you could call different tables and rooms, even the ladies restroom. Someone kept calling our phone and asking us if we wanted to use their hot tub.

"Um, I don't think so," I said.

"Don't you gorgeous young ladies want to have a bit of fun tonight?" said the voice. I glanced around the restaurant, unable to identify where it was coming from.

"Um, I think he wants to talk to you." I passed the phone to Letitia. She held the phone to her ear, laughed explosively, and hung up.

"Randoooom!" she said.

In the morning, we met up with Letitia again for a hike up Tunnel Mountain, the second easiest and most popular hike after Lower Falls. It was a popular trek for inexperienced outdoorspeople, but we kept having to take breaks, while fitter hikers stepped over us on the trail. At the top, there was a huge glass building. We sat inside and watched mountain goats eating the sparse flora growing between the rocks and boulders.

That evening, the three of us went to a British-themed pub that Letitia had heard about. It was full of young people sitting at shitty patio furniture. There was some sports game on a big TV.

We split a bottle of red wine, and then another. I became more relaxed with each sip, and after a while the music started to sound hypnotizing and Letitia's jokes became hilarious. As we poured from the third bottle, I was positively giddy. Peering across the bar, I made eye contact with this sporty looking guy with a long head. He was sitting with a group of equally sporty looking guys in soccer jerseys.

I turned back to face Letitia and Logan, before remembering Barb's magical eye contact trick. Logan and Letita were discussing how much they both wanted to travel to Japan. I nodded along, then looked back over to the sporty guy. At first, he wasn't looking, but then, perhaps sensing me watching him, he turned again to catch my eye. I turned away quickly. I meant to do it again, but I forgot all about him, and got caught up in an argument with Logan about whether cream cheese tastes good in sushi.

"I think it's so good!" I said.

"It's an abomination!" said Logan. "It's not how sushi was meant to be enjoyed!"

"Excuse me, is this seat taken?" We turned to see the sporty guy.

Oh God, I thought, with some horror.

"Uhhh," I said, turning to look at Logan and Letitia.

"Sure, why not!" said Letitia. Logan nodded.

"Weren't we just saying how great it is to meet new people on vacation?" said Logan, who was only slurring her words a little bit.

The guy beckoned to his friends to join us, and they dragged chairs from the next table and sidled up beside us on every side, shaking hands with Letitia and Logan, and smiling at me.

The sporty guy was named Freddie, and he actually was from the United Kingdom. I didn't find him very cute up close. He had an ugly haircut and intense eyes that made me worry he was on MDMA.

"I told my mates, I've got to sit by that one," he said, gesturing to me. "I just got such good energy from you across the bar."

"Hmmm, totally," I said, nodding and smiling at him, feeling my left eyelid droop.

He leaned in to whisper in my ear. "You like art and stuff, don't you? You've got that arty look about you." Across the table, Freddie's friend was holding Logan's hand. She was smiling bashfully, and fixing her gaze very intently at the table. Letitia seemed bored, nodding slowly and listening to another friend tell a long story, employing expressive use of his hands.

"Mmmm, yeah. I guess I am arty," I said.

"I love that," he whispered. "You're the most gorgeous girl here." I laughed meanly at this. Freddie's expression was lazy.

"Do you want to make out?" I asked. I didn't know why I said it, but I thought it was probably the attention, or the wine, or Roger trying to get me fired.

"What, like, here?" he asked, glancing around, almost giddily.

"I mean, yeah," I said. "But, if you don't want to, we don't have to." I turned away, pretending I wasn't interested anymore.

"No, no, I do! I do!"

"Okay." I stared at his mouth. He leaned in close to me, and slowly smushed his face into mine. He jammed his tongue inside my mouth. He pressed his torso against my body. It was massive, and shaped like an inverted triangle. I ran my hands through his hair. He moaned into my mouth theatrically.

I thought of all the people I would have preferred to kiss. I thought about Ivan, the blacksmith, who was married. I thought about Greg Chapman, or even Henrick. I thought about Daniel. Why was it so easy to get someone you don't care about to kiss you, and so hard to kiss someone you want?

We made out for what felt like ten minutes, before his kiss started to remind me of a suction cup on an octopus's tentacle. The alcohol turned in my stomach. I thought I was going to throw up. I pushed him away.

"You're beautiful," he whispered in my ear.

"Whatever." I wanted to put my head on the table.

"Can I see you tomorrow?"

"Absolutely not," I said.

"You're so mean," he said. "I love it."

"Whatever."

He pulled me in to kiss again.

"I've gotta stop," I said to him, pulling away. He kissed my cheek. He excused himself to go to the bathroom. I watched him turn the corner. When he was out of sight, I turned to Letitia and Logan.

"Let's go!" I said.

"Now?" said Logan.

"Yeah, we should go." I didn't wait for them to get up before going outside. I sat on a fancy bench made of stones, and put my head between my legs. My mouth felt enlarged, and full of someone else's saliva.

Letitia came out first. I raised my head. She was looking at her phone.

"I'm so sorry," I said. "I'm so embarrassed."

"What do you mean?"

"The guy I was making out with? In front of you?"

"I don't know what you're talking about!" she said, smiling innocently. Was pretending not to notice embarrassing stuff a social custom in Missouri?

"I'm just sorry if I put you in a weird position," I said, my eyes closed. "I shouldn't have made out with that guy."

"Look, do whatever you want," she said blandly, now rolling her eyes. She opened an app on her phone and took a selfie. Logan appeared, and we said goodbye to Letitia before heading back to the hostel on foot.

"Was I awful?" I asked Logan on the way. It was later than I thought, and the streets were mostly deserted.

"Oh my God, no, I thought it was funny!" said Logan. "You're so crazy, girl."

"I am such a slut," I said. I knew I was being annoying, but I was too drunk to care. "I'm so gross."

"You're not a slut, Josie. You're a good girl. A slut would have slept with him." Logan had such a sweet expression on her face.

"Wait, what?"

"Well, you didn't have sex with him, did you? So, you're not a slut!" she said. "Nothing to worry about. I'm not friends with sluts."

"But I would have been if I had?" That sounded awfully simplistic to me. Logan sighed deeply.

"Well, sadly, yes, that's, by definition, what a slut is. I was just trying to make you feel better by pointing out the flaw in your logic!"

"Is being a slut bad?"

"Of course it's bad. But that's not you!"

"But what if it had been?"

Logan paused. "But it's not!"

"Well, what about Ruben, is he a slut?"

"It's not the same when a guy does it."

"Are you serious?"

"I'm dead serious," she said. I didn't feel so drunk anymore.

"Is it bad when a man does it?"

"It's not the same," she said again.

"What's the difference?"

"Josie, I know about men. They don't see us, girls, as people right away. They'll do anything they can to have sex with us, and once we do, they're done with us. We have to make them see us as people before we let ourselves be physical with them, or else they will never ever think of you as anything but a piece of meat."

"How can all men be like that? What about Matt?"

"Why do you think we waited so long to have sex when we first started dating?"

"I don't understand." Now I really thought I was going to throw up.

"I'm friends with all sorts of guys, and you hear the things they say about girls, especially the ones that put out. We have to protect ourselves."

The words coming out of Logan's mouth were so dark and abject. I asked her more and more questions, and each answer confirmed to me that I had not misunderstood her. She was saying exactly what she meant to.

At the hostel, I looked in the mirror and saw myself doing the Kubrick stare. I adjusted my chin. I filled my water bottle and forced myself to drink the entire thing.

In the morning, my mouth was dry, and my eyes were itchy from sleeping with mascara on. I met Logan in the lobby, where she was eating a grocery store croissant from the complimentary breakfast bar. When I sat down, she beamed at me.

"Hey, sleepyhead!" she said cheerfully, appearing barely hungover. "How are you feeling?"

"Uhhhh, bad," I said. She laughed.

"Last night was *so fun*, though. And I loved our talk."

"You loved our talk?" I said.

"Yeah, it was so … deep."

"Deep? Really?" Nothing made any sense.

We drove to Lake Minnewanka, a quiet spot a few kilometres away. We went around the lake and sat on rocks, looking out the clear water and the mountains behind. There was a woozy sensation in my stomach and head, and I found myself examining Logan's face frequently. What else was in there?

"You okay?" Logan asked me at one point, reaching out a hand to rub my back.

"Yeah, I'm fine." We drove back to Banff and went for dinner at a Mexican restaurant. I kept surveying the men in the bar, searching for clues on their faces that they hated the women they were sitting beside or across from. I couldn't make anything out.

Neither of us heard from Letitia for the rest of the trip, but by the time we arrived back in Wells, she had followed us both on Instagram.

She posted a photo of the three of us at the top of Tunnel Mountain. *Had an amazing time with these ladies xoxoxoxo #banff #triplethreat*

Sooooo fun!!!! Come visit us in Wells! <3, I commented.

• • •

"You seem disturbed by your conversation with Logan," Barb remarked when I saw her next.

"I am disturbed, I guess."

"It can be disarming to hear that someone, a friend, has a radically different view on something as fundamental as sexual expression," she said.

"I think the scary thing to me is that we're actually the same, aren't we? We're afraid of men, and it underpins everything we do, even though we do such different things. I understand what she's doing, too. She's buying into how men see the world because it's better for her than not. Maybe I'd do that, too, if I knew how. Isn't that what I've been looking for?"

"I don't think you'd buy into it," said Barb.

"Well, we'll never know, will we?"

"You know, Josie, it might not feel like it all the time, but you do have some control over how you see the world."

"You're right, it doesn't feel like it."

"It takes time, too. It's not easy. But you can choose to see the good in people, and in men, if that's how you want to think about things. Logan maybe isn't one hundred percent wrong. We live under patriarchy, and there is an undercurrent of misogyny that runs through most things. We all live with that inside of us because it's all around us. That's upsetting to think about. But it's not everything."

• • •

I went to the cabaret at the end of the month. There, the improv troupe from the fall, with Greg, Jeremy, and their friends, performed a bunch of skits. They did a sketch about a guy being a creep on a date. Greg portrayed a second suitor, a nice nerd that the woman had rejected at first. Everyone laughed at the sketch, understanding that the creep was ridiculous and shitty, and that women should be treated well and not preyed upon by bad men. They all cheered when Greg's character humiliated the creep. When the group came out for the final bow, Greg blew a kiss to Millie, who caught it and pressed it to her heart. After, Oksana performed her folk dance, a headdress of flowers and ribbons adorning her head. We cheered for her.

I went home and wrote a story about watching the cabaret. I didn't think it was good enough for the Iowa Writer's Workshop, but I thought it was at least better than the skits.

Chapter 14

IT WAS AUGUST. SUMMER WAS STILL IN FULL SWING, BUT the weather was already becoming more like fall time. At night, the temperature almost always dropped to freezing. The whistle pigs, who'd once appeared under every bench and behind every garbage can, were suddenly gone, having dug their dens for another season of hibernation.

By mid-summer, I'd been able to pull the strings to close the gap in my corset completely. Agatha was right. The fat from my abdomen had been slowly pushed down into my hips over the course of the summer.

"I look just like Kim Kardashian," I said to Bobby, sticking my ass out in the mirror.

"You look the same as you always did," Bobby replied.

At work, I was bored with tourists, tired of saying the same things over and over again. I stopped trying to fill the silences that cropped up between us. They'd watch me expectantly, perhaps hoping I'd come up with some fascinating anecdote about the park, or a titillating historical fact. I never did. I watched, awestruck, as Jeremy energetically engaged with passersby up the street, strumming his little instrument and projecting his voice across the park like a real thespian.

One morning in the Wendle House, I found a mouse, dead and bloated, floating in the dirty dishwater from the previous day. I grabbed a dishtowel and brought it to the water, hoping to wrap up the body, but shrieked when it shifted under the towel. I ran outside, shuddering, and flagged down Henrick, who happened to be passing. He pulled the mouse out of the water easily and laughed when I turned away as he passed me on the way to throw it out the back door. He patted me on the shoulder as he left, and I wondered how he would tell this story to the other judges, and to people he saw around town.

Mike, Bobby, Logan, Daniel, and I spent our nights watching movies at the staff house or having bonfires behind the compound. Bobby had all but moved into the staff house since she and Mike had started dating. Hannah was not happy about this. She must have been pretty upset about it because she even complained about it to me.

"All I'm saying is that I can definitely hear the mattress creaking down the hall every night," she said, catching me alone in the kitchen one afternoon. "We miss *you* so much, Josie." Say what you will about me as a roommate, I could certainly not be accused of having too much sex.

"She's just mad that someone's having sex and it's not her," said Bobby after Hannah had left. Her arms were wrapped around Mike's waist, and they started kissing. Hearing the sloshing of their mouths meeting and coming apart again, I wondered if Hannah's ick wasn't entirely without merit.

. . .

Daniel's wife, Louisa, was coming soon. The date of her arrival snuck up on me, and a week from her visit, I found myself entirely unprepared to meet her. When Daniel spoke about his wife or slipped away from the group to call her in the evenings, she had only been a concept. I found myself becoming sentimental about the time I had spent with Daniel.

"You know," I said to him one night, just the two of us around the fire pit, "I'm really happy that Louisa is coming, but I'll be sad that we won't be spending so much time together anymore." I wasn't drunk, but I'd had two beers and felt brave. Daniel pretended that he didn't hear me, so I pretended I hadn't said anything.

"I wonder what kind of job I'll get for the fall," I wondered aloud, hoping to change the subject. "I know I want to come back and interpret next summer, but I can't decide whether I'll stay the winter here again. Maybe I'll move to Montreal again."

"Do you wanna go to Bowron?" Daniel said.

"Like, now?" I asked, startled by his abruptness.

"Yeah. I never got to go there much."

"I mean, yeah, sure, if you drive!"

"Deal!"

I sipped on a third can in the car as we drove, and, always the lightweight, I let my eyes open and close lazily as we rumbled toward the lake. The headlights of the sedan made the world look like trail cam footage.

We parked at the mouth of the lake. We couldn't see anything, and we ended up sitting in a patch of dirt just beside the water. There was nothing to illuminate the world around us but the moon and the stars, save for a few dim lights from the other side of the lake, revealing occupied cottages and small bonfires. The shadows of the mountains across the lake were black holes, sucking in light. Late-season bugs swarmed nearby, only their quiet but high-pitched hum giving them away.

I was tired and lay on my back. Daniel did, too, a few feet away. I told him that I used to know a lot of constellations and how to find them. Now, I only knew Orion's belt, which wasn't even visible this time of year, and the big and little dippers. I pointed out the dippers, but it was too dark for Daniel to see my finger. He started telling me about how, when he was a kid, his little brother would get so upset whenever he beat him at a game, so he just started losing on purpose.

I fell asleep while he was talking, and when I woke up he was talking about something else.

"Hmmmm," I said, trying to sound pensive in response to something he said.

"Were you sleeping?" he asked.

"Um, yeah. Sorry. I'm tired."

Daniel helped me to my feet and drove us back to the compound. I felt guilty for falling asleep, and guilty for telling him I would miss him, and for meaning it. He hadn't responded, which must have meant that I wasn't supposed to say it. Sometimes, I thought about Daniel all day, and the things we could do together and the things I wanted to tell him. It was strange to think I shouldn't. Sometimes, I imagined kissing him, or that I was Louisa.

"Well ... g'night," he said, handing me the keys in the parking lot. Under the fluorescent lights illuminating the area around the compound, our interactions, our trip to Bowron, turned sinister in my mind. I snatched the keys out of his delicate fingers quickly and turned to go inside.

"Night!" I shouted. My insides ached dully, as if they'd gotten too close to an open flame and been singed.

• • •

The next day, I visited the pub with Bobby, and found Daniel, Mike, and Logan already seated. They were talking to Janine, who was positively giddy about Louisa's arrival next week, and was leaning across the table and asking Daniel many questions about her.

"So, it's been a while for you, huh?" she said, raising her eyebrows. I thought this was a nosy question for someone who hated gossiping so much.

"Um, I guess you could say that," said Daniel politely. He was always good at answering annoying questions. He wasn't looking at me, and I was glad, because I didn't know what type of face I was making.

"So, you've been married for a few years. Next step, a family, right?" she prodded. "But maybe that's not something you've decided on just yet."

"No, actually, we have," said Daniel. "We're going to start trying as soon as we're together again."

My stomach was curdling. Daniel still wouldn't meet my eye, even as I stared at him. Why hadn't he told me this? We told each other almost everything.

I told everyone I'd left something at the compound and disappeared from them into my car.

I drove down the highway leading out of town, unsure where I could go that would appease the strange, painful sensations coagulating in my gut. My heart was beating fast, my mouth was dry, the various shapes of trees and bushes lining the road were swirling into an indecipherable discordant mass. I kept rubbing my nose, and soon tears came rolling down my cheeks and into my mouth.

I pulled over and cried for a long time.

I hadn't thought it was possible for me to develop feelings for Daniel because he was married. That was what had made him the perfect friend. But I had been sloppy and lazy. I cried because having feelings for Daniel, caring about him, made perfect sense. Nothing about it was a compromise, or a bet on his true character. I cried because there was nowhere to put all that I was overflowing with for him. If my heart was creaking open, as Barb said it would, what was on the other side of that door was disappointing, terrifying, and would only hurt me further.

I wished I had become Brandon's girlfriend, or Eddie's, when I'd had the chance, then none of this would be happening, and I wouldn't be feeling this way.

The worst part of it was that, in reality, nothing had happened at all. It was just me, and my emotions and wayward desire, creating trouble in a well-functioning world. Wasn't I always doing that? I had wanted to date Greg, I hadn't wanted to date Brandon, I had been frustrated with Logan, and Hannah, and Janine. I was presented with the same information and stimuli, but I reacted so differently than everyone else. Without me, wouldn't the world run perfectly smoothly?

I wanted to keep crying, so I put on "Send in the Clowns" by Judy Collins on my phone. When it was done, I played it again, this time putting it on repeat. It ended and started over again as I cried and waited for the swelling of the instrumentation to feel less satisfying, less painful. I turned the volume all the way up, glad that the passing cars and logging trucks would hear snippets of Judy's reedy, plaintive voice as they sped past. I wanted everyone to hear. I needed somewhere to put it all and hoped that passersby would take some of it from me.

I was scared that if I went back to the compound, I would knock on Daniel's door and tell him everything. He would fight me off as

I planted furious kisses on his face. Eventually, though, the crying did subside. I turned my car around.

In my room, I examined my puffy, red face. Soon, the swelling would go down, and my face would be normal again, and there would be no evidence of a problem. I was overcome with a sleepy, dull calmness and allowed myself to thoughtlessly drift into it.

• • •

Barb found the whole thing highly suspect.

"So, let me get this straight: this guy has been hanging out with you alone all summer, tells you he's proud of you, asks to go to Bowron alone with you in the middle of the night, to look at the romantic lake, all while being married to someone else?"

"Well, I knew he was married the whole time, Barb. And we don't hang out alone all the time."

"*And*," Barb continued, "he didn't tell you they were going to try for a baby? Something fishy is going on, Josie."

"Well, I don't know about that," I said. "Last week, I told him I was going to miss him when Louisa came and we wouldn't be able to spend as much time together anymore. I think it made him uncomfortable."

Barb scoffed. "Well, of course it did. Have you asked him how he feels?"

"Of course not. I could never do that."

"Because he's married?"

"Yes, because he's married. Besides, I don't think there's anything coming from his end. It's just me. I got too invested in our friendship."

"Josie, I'm sure Daniel is a nice guy. But he's also man. A man who is attracted to women. And he just got to spend the summer with a pretty young woman who isn't his wife."

"We're the same age," I said.

"Yeah, well." Barb waved her hand dismissively. "He's probably feeling the same way you are right now. Except he has a wife, so he doesn't have to worry about the fallout. You do. He's probably relieved she's coming, so he'll have an excuse to end whatever's been happening with you." I was shocked by Barb's flagrant disgust at Daniel. I thought she was just going to listen to me cry and tell me that love is a beautiful thing to want.

"I think this is just me, Barb." I tried to explain to her in a way that would make her understand. "I just misinterpret things. You know I haven't had many male friends before. I think I just can't handle it." I exhaled deeply, the weight of my failure washing over me. "I feel so guilty."

Barb paused. "You know, I'm hearing a lot of self-blame and self-loathing about something that isn't your fault. It's maybe not even Daniel's. You have feelings. You're a human being. It's incredibly normal, and common, to develop romantic feelings for someone you've spent a lot of time with. It's not unique to you, or life-alteringly embarrassing." She sighed. "What do you think would happen if you didn't level all these accusations at yourself? If you just let yourself experience your feelings, without worrying about whether or not you're doing everything right or without considering some hypothetical criticism that someone might have of you."

I thought about this. "I think … if I stopped checking myself for flaws, someone else would point them out, and I'd be caught unprepared."

"Is it possible you're missing out on opportunities for joy or spontaneity by being hypervigilant? We can't really control what people think of us or how they interact with us anyway."

"Maybe," I admitted.

"I don't think you should go into this situation feeling like a bad person. Just … do your best. It's going to be fine."

"Okay."

"Maybe you'll like her. Maybe you'll love her, and the three of you can navigate a new friendship together."

After therapy, I met Logan at Dairy Queen. I stared out the window, dumbly, and considered what Barb had said. Nothing was clear to me, but there was no action I could take to resolve my predicament.

"Are you okay?" Logan asked, eyeballing my ice cream cone as it melted onto my hand.

"Oh!" I said, reaching for a napkin. "Um, I'm okay," I said, wiping it up.

"You've seemed a little sad this week. You know, you can talk to me about anything."

We gazed at each other, her face angelic and kind. I had been so upset about what she'd said to me in Banff that I'd forgotten how sweet she was and how sure I was that she loved me. I loved her, too.

"I guess I've just been thinking about Daniel's wife coming to visit and have been a little bit confused." Tears pricked my eyes then, and I turned to stare out the window again.

"I was wondering if that was what was going on," Logan said. "I'm sorry to hear that."

"You were?" I asked. I couldn't believe it.

"Well, it's kind of obvious. You have so much in common, and you're both so great."

It was obvious? I swallowed. "Do I seem like I'm infatuated with him? Have I been embarrassing?"

"Not at all!" Logan said. "Not at all. I wasn't thinking about it like that. When Daniel told me about how you went to Bowron alone in the middle of the night I was like, 'You know what? Priests can sin, too.'"

"I don't think that's what was going on," I said, chuckling. "I genuinely think it's a one-sided thing. He's the least available person on the planet, essentially."

Logan shrugged.

I continued. "I'm nervous to meet Louisa."

"It's going to be okay. I'll be around. We can hang out while she's here."

"Okay," I said, smiling a little. How could Logan be so nice and also think that women who have casual sex are sluts? The world was full of mysteries.

Chapter 15

I AVOIDED DANIEL FOR THE REST OF THE WEEK. HE MOSTLY STAYED out of my way, too. When I did finally run into him outside the Wake-Up Jake, I was sure to mention how excited I was to meet Louisa.

"She's excited to meet you, too," he said. "I didn't realize this, but she's been sewing a dress all summer. A historic dress."

"Oh," I said, "that's cool."

"Yeah, she's going to join me on-site. I actually talked to Agatha last week, and she said it would be okay with her if she spent some time in Wendle House with you doing interpreter stuff. I know she'd love it. She's such a history buff, she's been reading about Barkerville and the gold rush all summer."

"Oh." I couldn't quite understand what he was saying.

"That's okay, right? If she works with you?"

"Oh, of course! Of course!" I repeated quickly. I ran to the bathroom in my dressing room and had diarrhea.

. . .

I didn't tell Bobby what was going on. I thought I could only tell her about it once I figured out how I could tell it in a way that would make her laugh. Otherwise, I couldn't predict how she would respond, or whether she'd tell Marcia. But nothing about it was funny to me, so I didn't say anything.

The day Louisa came I was working in the schoolhouse. During lessons, I watched the door obsessively, afraid Daniel would burst through the door, leading Louisa by the hand. I imagined the moment I'd see her for the first time and pictured myself falling to the floor, losing all of my faculties instantly, overcome with stress.

After work, I drove to the parking lot of the compound, where I found Daniel. He and Louisa were going to hitch a ride with me to the pub.

"Hi, Daniel, where is Louisa?" I asked, my voice formal as I climbed out of the car.

"Oh, she's inside, just grabbing a sweater." As he spoke, the door opened and Louisa appeared.

I had imagined Louisa many times, but she was different from every incarnation I had pictured. I realized then that Daniel had never actually described her to me physically before. She was much taller than him and had elegant shoulders and curly black hair that she'd pulled into a ponytail. Her sweater was bright blue and turquoise, and looked homemade. I thought she was beautiful.

She was silent as she approached me, her eyes fixed on mine. She drew me into a long, firm hug.

"I am so glad to meet you," she said. Her gaze was intense, but she smiled.

"I'm so glad to meet you, too," I said, smiling, too.

"Oh, shoot, I forgot my bag." She ran back inside unceremoniously.

"She's so beautiful and nice," I said awkwardly to Daniel.

"I … one hundred percent agree with you," he replied. We stood together, our arms crossed, and waited for her.

Going to the pub with Daniel and Louisa was less stressful than I expected. I found that I didn't have much time to stew, or consider the situation. Besides, Daniel and Louisa were a couple, but it wasn't like I had to watch them kissing or having sex. I didn't really have to think about it that much.

Daniel was bright and talkative with us, eager to point out that Louisa and I were both fans of *Anne of Green Gables — The Musical.* Louisa asked me if I wanted to join her Lucy Maud Montgomery reading group.

"We read theory and Canadian texts that were published around the same time as Anne. It's fascinating. I think you'll love it," she said. "Daniel is always saying how smart you are."

"Wow, that does sound fascinating," I said. I liked YouTube video essays explaining theory like you would to a five-year-old, but I could count on one hand the theory texts I had read and understood in university. After graduating, you couldn't have paid me to pick up a theory book.

"It's much more fun than bible study," Louisa said. I was taken aback for a minute. Daniel was technically studying to be a priest, but he never talked about it, or about God or Jesus at all. It was easy to forget he was religious. "Which this one avoids like the plague." She mussed up Daniel's hair. He looked sheepish. "Daniel hasn't finished a fiction book in like five years anyway."

"That Daniel," I said. "Always skipping out on bible study."

Something changed as the three of us continued to talk. They were so clearly a unit, and I came to understand that my feelings, ambiguous and abstract as they were, had no merit, no validity, against the living reality of a married couple. The two of them had had experiences and conversations together that I couldn't even guess at. I would never understand the depths of their tenderness toward one another, something deeper than physical touch or even words. I could never know, because I wasn't there when they met, or on their wedding night, or when they fought.

How could I move through this situation hoping to be the protagonist, the hero, when the happy ending had already happened, and I wasn't even involved? I was on the periphery, a side character who hadn't appeared until season four. My allegiances were shifting, and I heard myself making self-deprecating jokes, laughing at my stupidity and bad luck. I wanted them to like me, to invite me into their story, no matter the cost.

I was reminded of the way I felt in university when I lived with my friend Margot. We were the best of friends, and very similar. The main difference between us was that Margot was slightly better than me at everything, and in every way. She was a bit richer than me, a bit prettier, a bit thinner, ate a bit healthier. In groups, she knew just what to say. Boys that I liked developed crushes on her, and when I started going out with someone, I did everything I could to hide him from her, because I knew she could take him from me in a heartbeat.

After living with her for some months, I stopped imagining good things for myself. Anything that came my way would have been a waste. Margot would do better with it, whatever it was. I loved her, but moving away from her after I graduated was such a relief, and I eventually forgot how she made me feel and began wanting things again.

I was experiencing the same disloyalty to myself in front of Louisa and Daniel. Why shouldn't she have everything she wanted? She had earned it by being a strong, determined character. I wanted to disappear into their relationship, because existing in the world as myself was exhausting.

Logan, Bobby, and Mike appeared after some time and joined us. Logan and Louisa got into an argument about the film *Lady Bird*. Logan thought that the mother character was a good mom. Louisa thought the mother was abusive. I agreed with Louisa, and we nodded at each other in consensus, sisters in agreement. Logan threw her hands up, exasperated. Across the bar, the locals stole glances at us, curious to see Daniel's wife.

That night, as I lay in my lumpy bed, there was a perceptible emptiness, like there was a black hole in the centre of my chest, sucking the rest of my body into it. I got up and went to Bobby's room.

She opened the door, looking tired. She was holding an open bottle of moisturizer. I could see streaks of the white creamy liquid on her wrists. I climbed into her bed, accidentally upsetting her book, *Outlander*, which lay propped open haphazardly on her duvet. Her room was not the same as I had found it at the beginning of the summer. It was messy, and emptier, as she had transferred many of her belongings to Mike's room. It made me nervous to see, like I was peering into the messy recesses of Bobby's mind, learning what she did and didn't care about.

"I'm jealous of Daniel's wife," I said. Disclosure to someone was so refreshing and purifying, like turning to the first crisp page of a new notebook, even though I wasn't sure I could trust Bobby. After all, just the day before she'd told me Mike had the biggest penis she had ever seen, and I was sure that was meant to be a secret between them. Regardless, my desire for catharsis was stronger than my need for discretion. I would deal with the consequences come morning.

"Yeah?" she said. "She seemed a little ..." She trailed off, wiggling her fingers to imply strangeness.

"Really?"

"Um, yeah. And Marcia said she saw her arguing with Sharon about the price of her room. She said she didn't want to pay because she's only staying for two weeks!"

"Oh," I said. "That sounds … bad."

"Marcia said she seemed like a bitch."

"Oh." I wasn't sure how to process this information. On the one hand, wasn't I supposed to be Louisa's love rival? I knew, from a narrative standpoint, this counted in my favour. On the other hand, I was skeptical of everything Marcia said and hated the idea of agreeing with her.

"I feel out of control," I said. I told her about how I'd cried in the car. "Do you think it was wrong of us to spend so much time together this summer?"

Bobby yawned, and didn't answer.

"I guess I just need a boyfriend," I said.

"You'll meet a nice guy soon," said Bobby dopily, and she got under the covers and told me she had to get up early. I knew she wanted me to leave, but I didn't care. No force on Earth was more powerful than my need to expunge information.

"I just … need to figure out what's going on."

"Mmm. Listen, Josie, I have to get up at six."

"Oh, yeah, sorry, Bobby," I said. I closed the door softly behind me. Outside in the hall, it was all quiet, except for the hum of the machines keeping the fridges running and the heat working.

At the park the next morning, I found Louisa in full historic costume, chopping wood. She looked so beautiful. She grunted as she swung the axe, slicing each piece of wood neatly and assertively.

"Good day!" she said when she noticed me.

"Wow," I said. "I'm impressed."

"Well, I figure what's the point in even having this job if you're not going to do it, right?"

My cheeks warmed. "You're right." I said. Why hadn't I thought of it that way before? "Your dress is lovely," I added. It was lovely. That word came to me over and over whenever she was around. While my Victorian outfit had a Halloween costume-like quality to it, Louisa's truly seemed authentic. The hems and floral embellishments were lovingly stitched by hand, the colour a muted green that almost glowed amongst the historical buildings.

"Thank you. I'm sure you can tell but obviously" — she gestured to her skirts — "the design is a decade or two early." I couldn't tell. "But, of course, that would be normal for a woman in the Cariboo."

Between classes at the schoolhouse, I popped into the Wendle House, where Louisa was pulling a perfectly laminated rhubarb pie from the oven. Agatha sat at the kitchen table wearing a delighted countenance I had never seen before. The aroma was mouth-watering.

"I've never made a pie in here before. I didn't even know it was possible," I confessed.

"Are you kidding? You can do anything on this stove. You just have to use your imagination."

I sat and watched Agatha and Louisa have an in-depth discussion about historic cookbooks. Louisa had a collection, and she had spent hours poring over them as a teenager.

"You're a marvel," exclaimed Agatha, who looked ready to kiss Louisa. I frowned. I didn't realize Agatha could like someone this much. If I had known, I would have tried harder.

"I can't wait for us to work together tomorrow, Josie," said Louisa. "We can make my grandmother's coffee cake recipe."

"Oh, yeah. That sounds awesome."

"Is that okay, are you sure?" Louisa asked again, suddenly sounding concerned.

"Of course!"

After work, I found Daniel in the compound kitchen, sipping a glass of water and peeking at his phone. I was happy to see him.

"Where's Louisa?" I asked.

"Oh, she's napping. Jet lag."

"Ah," I said. "Are you having a nice visit?"

"It's been so great. Louisa really likes you."

"I really like her, too." It wasn't a lie. I did really like her, it just so happened that liking her wasn't the biggest feeling I had about her.

"Agatha likes Louisa a lot, too," Daniel continued. "And Louisa loved the Wendle House."

"Oh. That's nice."

"I'd be surprised if Agatha didn't offer her a job for next summer. Then she and I could be here together. That would be perfect for us. If we don't have a baby, of course."

My stomach sank to the soles of my feet. Before meeting Louisa, I hadn't thought critically about whether I was a good interpreter or not. I figured I was good enough, and the skills and knowledge I needed would come with time, and I would be even better next year. It was clear now that Louisa was a better fit for Daniel, and for my job. I remembered Agatha's face as Louisa presented the pie to her.

"That sounds nice for you two," I said.

We went to the pub to meet up with Logan, Bobby, and Mike again. I was quiet, penning an email to Agatha in my head where I could explain to her why I'm a perfect fit for the position again next year. I bounced my leg under the table. I furrowed my brow, trying to think of arguments as to why I was better suited for the job than Louisa.

When Louisa was in the bathroom, Daniel reached his arm across the table and placed a hand on my arm. He gazed at me intensely, with big sad eyes and his saddest, most sympathetic countenance.

Fuck off, Daniel, I thought. I could have smacked him. I imagined him with Louisa, later that night, so pleased with themselves, and so sympathetic to my situation, obsessed with a man I couldn't have, and bad at my job, to boot. I shifted my arm, moving his hand away. I glared at him.

"What's up?" I asked, privately daring him to ask me how I was feeling.

"Nothing," he said quietly, still smiling. He withdrew and joined a conversation Bobby and Mike were having about gramophones.

I did not sleep well that night. In the morning, my body was twitchy, and I had big bags under my eyes. In the middle of the night I opened my laptop and penned a long, pleading email to Agatha about my suitability to return to my job next summer, and how I'd only get better and more engaged with the unique and magical history of Barkerville.

Louisa met me in front of the Wendle House, carrying a big old recipe book.

"I have big plans today," she said with authority as I unlocked the door. She marched in ahead of me and planted the book on the table, opening it and flipping through the pages.

"Did you bring that from Montreal?" I asked.

"It was important," she said gravely. "Now, my grandmother's recipe calls for slightly soured milk. Do you have any?"

"Ummm," I said, opening the ice box and peeking inside. I wondered what would have had to change about my past for me to end up as the type of person who cherished her grandmother's coffee cake recipe. "We have regular milk?"

"Hmmmm," said Louisa. "Maybe instead I should just make another pie."

"That sounds nice," I said.

"I actually saw a raspberry patch behind the printing press yesterday, would you go and get me some?" She handed me a bowl. "I wanted to get started on laundry."

"You want me to go get you raspberries?" I asked.

"Well, yeah, I need them. Do you mind?"

"Um, no, it's fine," I said. My breath was becoming unsteady. "You know we just pretend to do laundry, right? We don't have to actually do it."

"Well, when will I ever have another opportunity to do laundry like it was done in the early twentieth century? I *have* to do it," she insisted emphatically.

"Oh, totally."

"Sometimes I feel like Daniel doesn't take enough advantage of this place, you know?"

"I guess so," I said, even though I suspected her standard was probably unfairly high.

I went to go collect raspberries, as if I was Louisa's ten-year-old daughter. I knelt behind the printing press and started grabbing berries to drop into the big metal bowl.

"Josie?" I heard a voice behind me. It was Bobby.

"Oh, hey, Bobby," I said.

"Woah, what's going on?" said Bobby when she saw my disturbed expression up close.

"Um, Louisa sent me to get raspberries for her pie."

"Wait, she sent you out of the Wendle House to get raspberries for her? That is audacious!" She sounded almost entertained.

"She is … something," I said, bitterly. "I thought we'd have tons in common, because me and Daniel have tons in common. But we're so different. She's so … good at everything."

"Being good at stuff doesn't mean you're not a bitch."

"Hmmm," I said.

"She seems intimidated by you, to be honest."

"I don't think so."

"Think about it. Why would she be sending you to get raspberries, like her servant? She wants to destroy you for spending the summer with her husband."

"I feel like she's been pretty nice, overall," I said. "Maybe a bit of a ... I dunno, know-it-all. But who isn't sometimes?"

"Then why haven't she and Daniel stopped talking about her being an interpreter in the Wendle House next year? They must know how that sounds."

My lip trembled. I bit it. "I guess I do think she wants me to know that she's better at this than me. But she's right. I feel rotten."

Bobby stayed and picked raspberries with me. We ate half, and put the other half in the bowl. After a while, Bobby stopped helping and lay on the grass, talking about Mike and his love of old-fashioned sodas.

Some time later, Daniel's unmistakable, pious silhouette approached, his black hat forming a dark halo around his head. I sighed, and Bobby made a face at me.

"Um, how's it going?" he asked.

"Fine," I said, sounding brusque. "I'm getting raspberries for Louisa."

"Great!" said Daniel. His voice was overly cheerful. "Do you think you'll, uh, head back soon?"

I stood up to glare at him. "What, did Louisa send you to come get me?"

I was angry.

"Um, yeah. She wants to go to the bathroom." Daniel looked at the ground.

"Fine," I said. Bobby scrambled to her feet, and we started back to the Wendle House together. Over my shoulder, I could see Daniel move to follow us. I quickened my pace.

"Okay, that was absolutely psychotic," said Bobby. "Sending her husband to fetch you?"

I had a horrible sense of foreboding as I returned to the Wendle House. There was too much emotion in the air. Bobby followed me inside, and I placed the bowl gingerly on the table. The back door was open, and Louisa was on the porch, scrubbing a petticoat over a washing board with her sleeves rolled up.

"Oh, excellent!" she said, approaching the bowl. "Hmmm, not quite as many as I'd hoped ... oh, hello." She noticed Bobby behind me.

"Heyyyy," said Bobby, cocking her head saucily.

"Well, sorry there weren't as many as you wanted," I said, with detectable sarcasm. I was flying too close to the sun.

"Oh, well, uh, that's okay," Louisa replied.

"Okay, what next?" I said, more carefully this time.

"Well, I need to go to the bathroom. Then I can get started!"

"The pie was delicious yesterday," I conceded, trying to recover both my mood and my capacity to be nice to Louisa.

"I'm so glad. I take great pride in my baking. I know when Agatha tasted it, she practically screamed 'you're hired!'"

Bobby whipped her head around to catch my eye, her mouth ajar, but not without a hint of amusement. I returned her gaze, aghast. We were silent. Louisa looked at us, bewilderment in her eyes.

When Louisa was gone, I burst into tears. Bobby closed the door to prevent any tourists from interrupting.

"What's going to happen to *me*?" I gasped petulantly, through sobs. Bobby's face was panicked.

"C'mon, it's okay!" she said, rubbing my back awkwardly. "At least you're pretty!" I kept crying. "Do you want me to tell Louisa you're not feeling well?" Bobby asked maternally.

I nodded my head.

"Okay," she said. "I'll go do that, but I have to go now, okay?"

"Okay," I said. "Thanks, Bobby." I wanted to wrap my arms around her waist and hold her there. I didn't want to be alone, but I let her go.

Tourists kept trying to open the door, sometimes poking their heads through the back window. I hid in the corner, wiping my tears and snot on dishtowels. I waited for the water to stop leaking out of my eyes. As soon as the tears subsided, they'd start up again at the memory of some humiliation I'd endured in the past few days.

There was a sound like a knock, but it was so quiet I couldn't be sure. A couple seconds later, I heard it again, more confident this time. I approached the back door, the floorboards squeaking under my boots.

"It's Daniel." His voice was cloying and anxious-sounding.

I opened the door. Seeing my tear-stained, puffy face, his boyish face became stricken, almost frightened. I sat down at the kitchen table, wordlessly. He shut the door and leaned against the frame.

We watched each other, waiting for the other to speak. The room was quiet, except for the sounds of my ragged breathing.

"I heard you had, um, an encounter?" Daniel said eventually.

I nodded.

"What, uh, happened?"

I narrowed my eyes at him. I knew without a doubt he'd already spoken to Louisa. "Well," I began, stopping to gasp out a little sob. It was all starting up again. "It seems as though" — another sob — "Louisa has been offered my job next summer by Agatha." "Agatha" came out like a screech.

Daniel made a pained, sympathetic face. I imagined him using that face on his parishioners when they told him their secrets. This enraged me.

"That must be hard," he said, nodding dutifully. "It can't have been easy news." He paused. "Does Louisa know?"

"She's the one who said it." I raised my voice. "I am mortified, Daniel. I am incredibly upset right now." It was a balm to name my feelings out loud. Once I started I wanted to keep yelling, but made myself stop.

"I see, I see." He stared at the floor as if deep in thought, considering this information carefully.

"*You* have to go now, because *I* have to stop crying so that I can do *my* job."

Daniel frowned. "I understand, I'll go now. I'm sorry."

"Please go." I said, although he was already out the door. I locked it behind him.

I hid in the shut-up Wendle House for an hour, replaying all that had happened in my head. I was searching for the moment that would prove that I was overreacting, or else the instance that showed Louisa and Daniel's poor character. But nothing was clear, and the more I thought about it, the more confused I became. At least there was the catharsis of what I had said to Daniel. I hadn't said anything untrue.

When I stopped crying, I visited Ivan at the blacksmith shop.

"Yama hama! What happened?" He asked when he saw my face. I told him.

"Agatha never would have said that," said Ivan. "Louisa was probably *lying*." Everyone was sold on the idea that Louisa was a bad person. Didn't they understand that she was Daniel's wife, and he loved her more than anyone? If she was a bad person, then the world didn't make any sense, because Daniel wasn't a bad person. There had to be another explanation.

"You really think so?"

"Absolutely. Agatha loves you! She talks about it all the time!"

"She does?"

"Sure!" I wished for a minute or two that Ivan was my sweet, old husband.

• : •

In my dressing room after work, I had a message from Louisa.

"Hi Josie, I'm truly sorry if I upset you today. I promise, I don't want your job. I never asked for it! I appreciate you letting me spend time with you in the Wendle House, and getting to know you better. You're Daniel's friend, and I want us to be friends, too."

Reading this, I was less certain than ever about what was going on. Still, I typed my reply.

"Hi Louisa, thanks for your message and for your apology. I really appreciate it, and don't worry about it — I think it was just a misunderstanding. I'm really happy you're here, and I've loved getting to know you. I hope we can still spend time together, but maybe not in the Wendle House ha ha!"

I deleted and retyped "and for your apology" six times before sending the message, and "I think it was just a misunderstanding" four times.

Louisa responded with a laughing emoji two minutes later.

After work, I went straight to the staff house to find Logan. I explained everything, trying to avoid slipping any overly salacious commentary into it.

"She did what?!" Logan yelped.

"I think it was just a miscommunication," I said, resting my chin on the kitchen table.

"Still, that's wacko, girl. You showed her." She shook my shoulders gently.

• • •

"We had a conflict," I told Barb when I saw her two days later.

"You and his wife?"

"Me and Louisa, yeah." I told her everything.

"I'm shocked. You have to have pretty big balls to stroll into Barkerville and expect to work as an interpreter, just like that."

"I think I was just playing the victim," I said. "I was the one who created the problem. No one was upset before I started crying."

"In what way were you being a victim?" she asked.

"Well, I cried. Daniel had to 'handle' me."

"I mean, you stood up for yourself. You didn't let her back in when she crossed a line. You told the truth when Daniel asked you. They were trying to walk all over you."

I wasn't sure if I trusted what Barb was saying. She liked me, and wanted to support me.

"I don't know if that's true," I said. I genuinely didn't.

"And where is Daniel in this conflict? He comes to you, not to comfort you, but to do recon for his wife?"

"I guess."

"I'm not guessing. That's what happened. This person acted like your friend, and then let his wife bulldoze you."

"But I'm in love with Daniel. Or I thought I was. Why shouldn't she bulldoze me? She's his wife. She should run me over with a bulldozer."

"Josie, you didn't create this problem by having private, complicated feelings for Daniel."

I shrugged.

"No. Josie, you didn't do this. Do you understand?"

"I dunno."

"No, Josie, you didn't create this problem. The problem walked into your place of work and made a pie."

Chapter 16

AFTER MY DISCUSSIONS WITH BARB AND LOGAN, I REALIZED I wasn't actually mad at Louisa at all. I was surprised to realize that I didn't have that many thoughts about her at all.

When I returned to work, she visited me in the schoolhouse between lessons, wearing her modern clothes, as if surrendering the realm of history to me.

"I sewed my shirt myself," she explained when I complimented her on it.

We didn't really talk about what had happened, but instead discussed *Anne of Green Gables* and what she wanted to name her future babies. She complained about Daniel, and I laughed with her about his shortcomings and idiosyncrasies. It was a relief to be friends. This time, there was a deflated, calm quality to our interactions, like our encounter had poked a hole in the inflatable mattress of our relationship.

I avoided Daniel. I was mad at him, I came to understand. I treated him icily when I ran into him at work or on the compound.

"Louisa's inside," I'd say, pointing to the door when he came around, his demeanour jittery. It was four days before he approached me directly.

"Can we have tea tonight? Maybe in your room?" he asked formally.

"Fine," I said.

"Eight?"

"Yeah, fine."

He appeared at my door with two mugs of hot water and teabags in his pocket at eight sharp. I stood aside and let him in. I reached for my mug, happy to see it wasn't shaking in my hand. We made nervous small talk about the weather, and how the summer season was coming to an end.

"I'm disappointed in you," I said to him finally.

"I know," he returned.

I took a deep breath. "Daniel, I know you're married and your relationship with Louisa is the most important relationship you have. I understand that." I could hear myself forming coherent sentences. "But I feel like you let, or you encouraged, Louisa to come into my working space in a way that wasn't appropriate. It hurt me that you said you hoped that Louisa would have my job next year. I had a great summer with you, and it was hard to hear that. It's also my job, and it belongs to me."

"I understand," said Daniel. I was shocked by how easy this was. "And I don't want you to lose your job." His words rang almost sincere.

"Okay."

"I am sorry, Josie."

"It's okay," I said. I couldn't remember the last time someone had apologized to me.

"And I'm also sorry," he continued, "that I haven't been able to, you know, hang out as much, since, you know." He shrugged, and averted his eyes.

"No," I said, as firmly as I could manage, "that's not what this is about." The last thing I wanted was Daniel coming away with any sense of having hurt me romantically. I couldn't bear the humiliation.

Daniel stayed in my room with me. We joked around, and he did his Gollum impression for me. I appreciated it, but I could tell he wanted to leave, to be with Louisa.

He gave me a big hug at the door as he left. We exchanged warm words of goodbye, affirming our friendship and how happy we were to know one another.

When I was alone, everything was different. The romantic affection I had held for Daniel was gone, or at least fundamentally changed. I understood definitively that the closeness we had shared was over. I would miss it, but I wasn't sure if I wanted it back. A dull, tender loneliness washed over me. I went to bed.

I was happy that things were settled between me and Daniel and Louisa. I could tell people around town were talking about it, because Lyle Smith, the interpreter with award-winning chili, kept approaching me and asking me to have an affair with him.

"I just want you to know that if you're looking for a steamy, hot extramarital affair, I'm right here, baby!" he said, cornering me at the pub one evening. He licked his lips.

"Um, no thanks," I said, slipping away.

• • •

Everyone was leaving. August was nearly over, and Mike and Daniel needed to return to school. Logan, too, was nearing the end of her contract and would be gone within weeks. Soon, it would just be Bobby and me, waiting out our contracts.

In the meantime, Louisa grew sick of interacting with tourists, and she stopped hanging out in town with Daniel during the work day.

"They just say the same things over and over again!" she said, exasperated.

"I know, right?" I agreed. Perhaps we were on more equal footing than I'd initially thought.

Agatha finally responded to my email and wrote that she would be happy for me to return next year. I responded, and said I'd love to return, although the idea of humouring guests every day for another one hundred days made me sweat.

Nancy emailed me, too. She told me there was a contract to work in the archives for the winter that would begin in October, right after the summer season ended. It was mine if I wanted it.

I was torn. I had been hoping that someone would ask me to stay longer, hadn't I? I wanted someone to want me, and now someone did. I thought about the comfy bed in the staff house, the long drives to Quesnel, the snow, the quiet, and Barb. I loved the Cariboo, didn't I? But then again, Logan would be gone, and Bobby, and Daniel. I'd have to hang out with Hannah all winter, and Armand, and whoever the next government-subsidized intern was.

I left the email in my inbox for a week before telling Nancy I couldn't take it.

"Our loss," wrote Nancy. "Best of luck to you."

I started to apply to other jobs, ones in cities around Canada. I had an interview at a law firm in Montreal, who offered me a position as a legal assistant, to begin in early October. I liked the idea of law. I thought it would have an immediacy that struck me as the opposite of working with history. History would always be there, as would the financial and bureaucratic barriers preventing the government from funding it properly. Besides, I knew I'd quit in spring to come back to Barkerville. I felt less confident about my abilities as an interpreter than ever before, but I was committed.

"We can see each other all the time," said Daniel when I told him the news about my job.

"You're right," I said. "We can keep watching *Mad Men*."

As August came to a close, Barkerville began to resemble the place it had been when I arrived almost a year earlier. The few deciduous trees turned fiery reds and yellows, and the tourists thinned out until there were mostly only Germans.

"I see you have a kitty!" said one such German to me in the schoolhouse on Sunday, pointing behind me.

"Huh?" I spun around. There were no cats in Barkerville.

"It's tail, I saw its tail!" she said. "It went into the next room." Peeking my head around the corner, I saw a slithery, shiny tail slip up between a tiny gap in the wall I hadn't noticed before. Dougie, who had picked up a gig working park maintenance, pulled the creature out of the nook and showed it to me.

"A marten," he said, cradling the animal with surprising tenderness. It squirmed and hissed in his arms.

Checking the residents out of the compound was very satisfying. Since the meeting in July, I had effectively been absent as the camp caretaker. This didn't matter so much, because everyone had decided to do their dishes for the rest of the summer. I assumed this was either because they didn't want to violate the health codes, or they felt guilty that I had cried in front of everyone. John had pivoted to kissing my ass for the remainder of his stay, while Roger and Riley behaved as thought there was never any animosity between us.

"Well, see ya," said Roger, as he handed me his keys. I didn't say anything back, but he didn't notice at all.

The residents were abuzz with expectation and hope as they checked out of the compound. Most of them were going to college or university and were no doubt imagining what life had in store for them next. Their mothers, who came to pick them up, placed their hands gently on their children's heads and shoulders. After all, they were just children at the end of the day.

• • •

Saying goodbye to Louisa and Daniel was strange, because I was moving to Montreal, where they lived. Technically, we could see each other all the time come October. I wasn't quite sure if this would actually happen, or if I wanted it to, but it prevented things from getting too emotional, and I was grateful. Louisa gave me another impressive hug, while Daniel embraced me weakly, which I supposed was all he could muster under the circumstances.

Bobby was devastated when it was Mike's turn to leave. She hid her sniffles from me poorly as we watched his dad drive him away and back to Kelowna.

"I'm gonna move to Kelowna this fall," she said, her eyes shiny. She said it like a solemn vow. "This has been the best summer of my life."

I drove Logan to the airport the week after. It was strange to tack her departure on at the end of Daniel's and Mike's, because I'd known her for so much longer. It was like a different category of goodbye altogether.

In the car, we were quiet. There wasn't much to say. The things we had in common would soon be things we didn't have in common, when her home was back in Vancouver, with Matt. I tried to think of some summarizing thing to say about the year, some life lesson. But I wasn't sure I'd learned any lessons.

We hugged for a long time at the Prince George airport, and promised to talk all the time. I could tell she was happy to be leaving Wells, and leaving me, and I tried not to take it too personally.

"I'm happy for you," I said. "I'll miss you."

"You have fun in Montreal," she said. I watched her enter the big glass doors and disappear around a corner. On the car ride home, I remembered all the things we had done together, things that had eluded my memory as we were saying goodbye. At one point we had been like real sisters, and for a minute my chest ached for that time.

I returned to the mostly empty compound in late afternoon. The sun was now setting earlier and earlier, and weak light fell through the windows on either end of the long hallway, which was cavernous now and hollow now. I knocked on Bobby's door, and we spent the night watching *Twilight*.

There were three and a half weeks left in our contracts. The sudden drop-off of the Wells population left Bobby and me manic, searching for stimulation. Lonely without Daniel and Logan, I sought her out whenever I could. A lot of the time, she was with Marcia. When we were together, she was distracted and surly. I planned movie nights for us, day trips to Quesnel on our days off. I'd notice her eyes glaze over as I spoke, her nods becoming absent minded.

"I mean ... I kind of just want to go to bed tonight," she'd say. I begged her to watch *Outlander* with me. "Just one episode?"

I enticed her on a hike on one day off, but not even the great outdoors lifted her mood.

"You know, Marcia was confused by your new job," she said, crankily.

"My new job? What do you mean?"

"Well, she just said it was dumb that you have two degrees, a master's in archaeology, but you're going to be a *legal assistant*." She pronounced "legal assistant" with disdain. I wondered if that was how Marcia said it.

"Wow, Marcia must really hate me."

"Well, I dunno," said Bobby, who started to laugh. "I'm kind of on a gag order here."

"What? What do you mean?" I had just been expecting her to say "No, of course she doesn't!" and found myself unprepared for another answer.

"Well, yeah. She doesn't like you. She says you annoy her. She said it's just something about you that makes her angry."

"Oh," I said. We were quiet. My heart was in my throat and I was breathing out of my mouth. Bobby walked ahead of me, and I watched her step capably over rocks and fallen trees. We'd spent so much time together over the summer. Had she just been reporting to Marcia the whole time, about all the things I was doing? I replayed all of the secrets I'd told her, about Hannah, about Janine, about Logan and Daniel. I considered all of the qualities I hated about myself the most and wondered which ones had made Marcia dislike me.

"But," she blurted out suddenly, "she did say, just last week actually, that, uh, she doesn't feel that way anymore! She changed her mind." Her lie was so obvious that it stung. I was quiet for the rest of the hike, suddenly zapped of energy. She didn't appear at my room in the evening, and I didn't knock on her door.

My last meeting with Barb was anti-climactic. It was strange to meet to say goodbye, a week before my actual departure. My brain couldn't understand it, or muster any of the appropriate emotions.

Still, she gave me a once-in-a-therapeutic-relationship hug, and told me we could do virtual therapy if I wanted.

"That would be nice," I said.

"Take care, Josie," she said, squeezing me softly. "I'll miss talking to you."

I had expected some big speech from her, tidily summing up my growth. How else was I supposed to know if I was better than I'd been before? I wanted a certificate of mental health that I could display in my bedroom or home office, but I left empty handed.

I sold my car to Henrick before I left town. It had cost me eight thousand dollars, but he would only pay three thousand.

"That's all I can do." He shrugged. I wondered if he got away with lowballs like this all the time because he was handsome. In the end I accepted the offer.

Handing the keys over was an emotional affair. Somehow, I needed the car to go to someone I was sure had a rich inner life. How was I supposed to know whether Henrick had one? Before making the trade, I admired my beautiful Chevy Cruze one last time. It was my first car, and I had loved every minute of driving it. I wanted to lean down and hug it across the hood, but I was in the Barkerville parking lot, so I left it.

Bobby had found a studio apartment on a vacant vacation rental property in Kelowna. We ended our respective contracts on the same day, so we agreed that I would book my flight from Kelowna, and we would drive down together in her pickup. The previous day, Bobby had been at a cultural heritage conference in Prince George. I was hitching a ride to Quesnel with Rhoda, but before I did I ran into Hannah.

"You're leaving? Already?" she said, almost panicked. "We'll miss you so much."

"I am," I said. "But I'll be back. Next spring."

"It won't be the same without you."

I studied Hannah. When I lived with her, I was so afraid of being like her. But now, seeing her from afar all summer, that fear was so remote, and it was hard for me to even remember why I'd felt that way.

"I hope you have a really good winter," I said. We smiled at each other.

Rhoda took me to town and dropped me off at the A&W. I appreciated the lift, but it was sad to experience my final drive into Quesnel on someone else's terms.

Bobby was late to meet me. After an hour, I frantically texted her all manner of things, bouncing my leg under the table. "Hey, are you coming?" "Hey, if you don't wanna do this I can still buy a ticket from Quesnel, just please let me know." I ate a Chubby Chicken burger, a large order of fries, and an order of onion rings.

When she finally arrived, two hours late, her demeanour was equal parts manic and sullen. "Sorry! Sorry! Marcia didn't want me to go. She said it would be rude for me to leave before every presenter had gone."

"Oh," I said. "That's okay." I threw my bags in the bed of the truck. She was so flustered that I thought it would have been cruel to lecture her. Besides, I didn't want to say anything that she could report to Marcia.

Our drive was quiet. We shared small comments with each other, reflecting on the summer, how fun it had been. I was wary of saying too much, of embarrassing myself. Watching her drive, I couldn't tell if I knew her at all.

We arrived in Kelowna at 10:30 p.m. Bobby wanted to stop at Mike's house before we headed to her apartment. He was going to give us an air mattress to sleep on.

"Don't worry, we won't be long," she assured me, grinning sheepishly at me.

Mike lived in the suburbs with his parents, in a pristine little house that didn't remind me of him at all. Inside, Mike and Bobby started making out, and I tried to avoid looking at them. I sat on the couch beside them for a long time, discomfort spreading through my body like wildfire.

"Oh my God, you really don't want to be here, do you?" Mike laughed, catching a glimpse of my face as he came for air. He readjusted his position so he was sitting up straight and facing both of us. "So, how were the last weeks?" he asked.

"They were okay, although I think I was getting on Bobby's last nerve," I said, turning to her and nudging her gently.

"Um, no comment," said Bobby, avoiding my eye. She kissed Mike. My mouth twisted into an uncontrollable frown. I could feel the sticky, sore feeling in my throat, threatening tears. Thinking back, I wondered how I had managed to establish a friendship with someone who now seemed to hate me so much.

"Marcia's coming to town, eh?" she said as she pulled away, nuzzling her face into his neck. Mike was excited about Marcia's visit, and described his favourite brewery, where they would visit, and the best restaurants. Bobby started to tell Mike about the job interviews she had lined up, which ones where her favourite, and how wonderful it would be when she was employed, and how they could work toward building a life together. More kissing.

"Um, do you think we can go soon?" I asked, when I couldn't wait any longer. Bobby sighed deeply.

"Okayyyyy," she said, making her voice sound like a baby's. She clung to Mike's chest and pouted at me. I stared back, too tired to make my face do anything but what it was already doing. "Fine," she said, in her regular voice.

• • •

Back in the car, Bobby was kinder with me. Maybe she was less brave without her boyfriend. "Sorry that took so long," she said, sounding genuinely contrite. "It was just so nice to see him."

"It's okay. I'm just tired. Let's go."

Bobby's apartment was a small room with a kitchenette overlooking a lake.

"The lease doesn't cover the summer, but it's pretty nice, right?"

"It's very nice," I said.

Bobby unwrapped Mike's air mattress, and we waited for the air pump to inflate it. I closed my eyes and leaned my head against the wall.

"Oh, no," I heard Bobby say a minute later.

I opened my eyes. The mattress was inflating, but it was undeniably a twin. "Shit," she said.

"Oh, God," I groaned. I buried my face in my hands. We sat among her belongings. My head was ringing. I couldn't believe this.

"Well, maybe you can sleep on some of my clothes? We can make a pile!" said Bobby. "You can use my comforter?"

"Absolutely not," I said, eventually. "I'm going to a hotel." I stood up.

"Wait, are you serious?" said Bobby.

"Yup." I collected my suitcases.

"Wow, okay. You're really going." There was a panic rising in her voice.

"I'm gonna call a cab." I pulled out my phone and opened Safari to search for a taxi company.

"Well, I mean, I can *drive you*," she said. "I'm sorry. It was stupid Mike's mattress."

"It's fine." I just wanted to go to bed.

She drove me to a retro but clean-looking Super 8 motel sandwiched between two near-identical establishments.

"Well, goodbye, Bobby," I said. "It was nice spending time with you this summer." I wished I wasn't so tired, and that she hadn't been so awful at Mike's house, so that I could properly assess what type of goodbye I wanted to give her.

"Can I at least drive you to the airport tomorrow?" she asked. Her face was pleading.

"You really don't have to," I said, averting my eyes.

"I want to. I do, I swear."

"Well ... okay, if you want to." My voice was flecked with just-detectable sarcasm.

At the motel, I slept like a baby. The room was perfectly temperature-controlled, my bed just the right size. When I woke up, I was a new woman, refreshed and ready for the journey ahead, and confident that I had been too hard on Bobby.

Bobby was also in a good mood when she met me in the parking lot.

"You look ... refreshed," she said as I wheeled my big suitcase toward her. She lifted it into the bed, and I tossed in my smaller one.

"Thanks so much for driving me," I said. I was glad we were going to have a friendly goodbye, because I liked her so much. I thought about how charming she was, and how all of the curatorial staff liked her, and found her sweet and funny.

As she drove me to the airport, she told me about her job interview in the afternoon at an outdoor sports store.

"That's the perfect job for you!" I said.

"Right?" She was beaming. I was excited for her new life, even if she forgot about me.

Pulling into the terminal, Bobby hoisted my bags out of the back, and we wheeled them onto the landing in front of the sliding doors.

"Bobby, thank you for a really fun summer," I said, my voice formal. "I hope you find the perfect job, and have a great winter with Mike."

"Thaaaanks!" she said, somewhat awkwardly. "I ... hope you get a boyfriend, and that he's, uh, really nice to you." She was grinning widely, but not the kind of grin that implied fondness.

"Oh," I said, taken aback. "Thanks. Bye." We looked at each other, and I hesitated a moment before moving to pass her, my suitcases bumping together as I pulled them behind me. I entered the airport through the sliding doors and didn't look behind me.

On the plane, with a tiny plastic cup of Sprite in my hand, I considered what had happened. It was surreal to think that that was my last goodbye in British Columbia, and my last conversation with Bobby, maybe ever. Was this the sum of my relationship with her? Was it the sum of my time in Wells? I didn't know. I closed my eyes and reclined in the seat. For once, sitting there, inhaling the recycled air, my mind was blank, my thoughts quiet. I listened to the hum of the engine outside and gripped the armrest as we took flight. All around me were ordinary people, fixed securely in the twenty-first century. Their concerns lay in the present, and the future. *Mine should, too*, I thought to myself.

When I arrived in Ontario, I emailed Agatha and told her I wouldn't be returning.

Acknowledgements

A big thank you to my parents, Carol and Dennis Teed, and siblings, Maddie, David, and Kate, for their support throughout the publication process. I'd like to thank the Dundurn team, particularly my editor, Julie Mannell, who makes my dreams come true, as well as Jess, Erin, Alyssa, Elena, Sara, and Jenny. Thanks to Fawn Parker for her mentorship and insight. Thanks to my friends Ana, Aishwarya, Una, Rebecca, and Julie for their eyes and ears. I'm also grateful to my former boss, Mary Keyork, and the team at Keyork Immigration Law, for their flexibility and support of my writing, and to my new boss, Tiziana, for the same. Finally, thank you to the employees of Barkerville Historic Town and Park, past and present, who offered me their historical knowledge and insight.

About the Author

Josie Teed was born and raised in Pelham, Ontario, and attended McGill University before completing her master's in archaeology at the University of York. Her work has been published in *Bad Nudes* and *Graphite Publications*. She lives in Montreal, Quebec, with her cat, Pepper. In her spare time she enjoys watching *Murdoch Mysteries* and going out for all-you-can-eat sushi with her siblings.